per amore

GIORGIO ARMANI

per amore

RIZZOLI
NEW YORK

New York Paris London Milan

"Growing means adapting the perfect world of ideas to the imperfect world of reality. It takes a lifetime to do so, but you'll succeed in the end."

Giorgio Armani

Several years ago, on the occasion of the fortieth anniversary of the brand and the company that I founded, I decided, after some initial hesitation, to publish a special book in which the events and images of my life, rather than the people, would be the main characters. That way, I would avoid the danger of mentioning one person while omitting another who was equally deserving. I began to wonder whether or not I wanted to tell people the story of my life. I doubted that even a person who loves my designs would really want to know anything about my childhood, or how I got started, whether it were deeply personal facts about myself or just the same old official information. The book was a success. The sequence of images arranged in nonchronological order to underscore the long-lasting nature and the timelessness of my vision of style struck a chord in readers. Even more so, the words I used in the book were appreciated: the story of the events concerning my family, told all in one breath, and a series of texts on my way of being, of living, of working—bywords that constantly recur in my way of doing and thinking. Although I am not dogmatic, in practice I always discover myself to be coherent.

Today, I am going back over those writings, because I think they can be useful to many, in different ways. To those who want to work in fashion, perhaps, but also to those who are just curious. Since 2015, the year this book was first published, to the present time, many things have happened in my profession. Telling them is easy: these are chronicles to be consigned to the annals of history. Of much greater importance is what has happened to the world that has involved all of us. The pandemic was an alarm bell, a wake-up call. No one was left unaffected. I thought a great deal and acted quickly, finding myself close to people as never before. This closeness led me to rethink this book, to enrich it, turning it into a very personal document: one of commitment, devotion, vision. Fashion may be the backdrop, but what it really talks about is life.

The invitation once again is to read it by skipping from one byword to another, without following a specific pattern. At the beginning the reader will find my complete biography, as told by me. This is my story. These are my values.

Enjoy.

PORTRAIT OF GIORGIO ARMANI, 1994

ME, IN MY OWN WORDS

I WAS BORN IN PIACENZA,
ON THE BANKS OF THE RIVER PO

I was born on July 11, 1934, in Piacenza, a city on the banks of the River Po whose origins go back more than two thousand years. I remember it as a peaceful town, not that far from Milan, a city whose endlessly fascinating presence could always be felt. I liked living in the province: the countryside was nearby, the food was good, and everything had a familiar feel. There were friends, at first with whom to share the games children play; then, later on in life, with whom to begin to know a bigger world. Unless families were quite well-off, they could not afford to own a car, much less a telephone, which was then a heavy, clunky, black object. The only place you could see a white phone was in the movies, which were, in fact, called "white telephone films." It was many years before I used a telephone for the first time; I remember it being an unfamiliar and awkward experience.

GIORGIO ARMANI AT THE AGE OF EIGHT,
THE DAY OF HIS FIRST COMMUNION, 1942

My brother, Sergio, was born five years before me; Rosanna was born three years after me. We lived a simple but quiet life until the war broke out. My father was hired to work as an office clerk at a local Fascist headquarters. In those days, working for the regime was almost self-preservation, because if you weren't part of the regime, you weren't looked on favorably; it could even be dangerous.

The Istituto Luce's feature films and political propaganda had a huge impact on everyone at the time (although I remember thinking that those films didn't seem to match the reality of our day-to-day existence). We abided by the rules of the regime but held very different beliefs; my parents, like many others, secretly listened to Radio London. I was too young to fully comprehend it all, as I didn't understand why my parents would want to pay attention to those responsible for bombing our cities. Political propaganda unquestionably influenced many young men, drawing them to great public gatherings where everyone wore a uniform, which gave a sense of belonging, and gymnastics events, which exalted one's physical performance and promoted the kind of superiority that led one to feel he could conquer the world.

My brother and I were very young when my father took us to visit the Federale. I still remember that office, filled with black pennants and decorated with painted, sculpted, and even embroidered skulls. But the whole scene wasn't convincing to me, somehow, and I left that headquarters with my mind filled with doubts. Sergio, already being a young man, had become involved with the regime, to the point that he joined the special Fiamme Bianche (White Flame) squads. My mother hardly managed to dissuade him.

My father was a taciturn man for whom it took very little to look elegant—as people would say back then—whenever he didn't have to wear his uniform. But I always picture him, even now, in that Fascist uniform: a black jacket made of coarse woolen cloth, baggy blue-gray gabardine trousers, a black tie over a black shirt. How curious: isn't there something about the description that reminds us of the way people dress today? He loved the theater, but especially whodunits, French noirs, and American movies, which then were of great formal elegance. I was not able to share my doubts to him about the regime—the truth is, at first I felt he was too aloof for me to be able to confide in; later, I thought he was too absent-minded, which made me feel as though I would have to face life all on my own. Vivid memories of him still appear in my mind. I remember perfectly well the moment he would open a metal box, like a small safe, and take out, counting them one by one, thousand lire banknotes—large, ruby-colored ones—with us children all around him, as though he wanted to reassure us of the fact that our finances were solid. He loved soccer, and he had even played the game when he was younger. He also loved the horse races at San Siro and the car races at the Velodromo Vigorelli. He died too young. I was just twenty-five, and it seemed I had never really known

GIORGIO ARMANI'S PARENTS, UGO AND MARIA
ARMANI, WITH HIS SISTER ROSANNA, 1942

PORTRAIT OF UGO ARMANI, 1957

him. I don't think I ever imagined that I'd write about him in the sort of autobiography you're reading now.

My mother's name was Maria Raimondi. Maìn when she was a child, Mariù as a young woman. I gave these two nicknames to my boats, as if I wanted her to participate in a life that we could never have imagined. My mother's first trip over water was on her honeymoon, for just a few hours, sailing on Lake Como. My mother and father had met on the stage of the Filodrammatica in Piacenza, when they were both acting in Henrik Ibsen's *A Doll's House*. They hardly ever mentioned their artistic past, perhaps out of a sense of modesty. The theater was, to some extent, in my family's blood, and not just because my paternal grandfather had a small workshop that made wigs for the Teatro Municipale, our own somewhat smaller version of the Teatro alla Scala. I was absolutely mesmerized by the atmosphere of the theater—the lights, the costumes, the anticipation as the curtain rose, not a sound coming from the audience. The small town of Piacenza was once transformed right before my eyes into a great Paris, a place I had never been to. It was while I was attending the staging of *La Bohème*, whose set was filled with candle-lit gables, that I realized I was taken more by this created world than by the singing of the artists. I was struck by the fact that as the artificial snow was falling upon the stage (according to the script), it really was snowing outside, coating the small nineteenth-century square opposite the theater. My brother shared this same passion for the theater.

He was very gifted; he could draw comics and make up stories that came to life through the marionettes he juggled with his hands, giving each one of them a different voice as he told their story. He even invented a radio station that each night, in the silence of our bedroom, would put on a play. And each night, just as the story reached its climax, he would end it right at that moment! While that would understandably make me furious, I was captivated. Nowadays, it takes a lot more than that to amaze a child. Our ingenuity reached a peak when we were asked to put on a show in a parish church in the countryside near Piacenza. We took care of everything, even "printing" the tickets. We made two hundred of them, perfect down to the smallest detail: perfectionism was always a must in my family.

My mother never talked about her past—about how, when she was still very young, she had to take care of her family after her own mother and three siblings died of the Spanish flu that had plagued Europe, not unlike Covid-19 that has so overwhelmed all of us. Although it unquestionably took a toll on her, it also prepared her for life's ups and downs. She looked after us and, whenever she was free from family duties, she'd carry out certain official tasks that were assigned to her as the person in charge of the local Dopolavoro, one of the workers' recreational clubs that cared for soldiers wounded in the war as well as their families.

My mother's true character came out one day when the patroness on duty during a visit to the hospital wanted to attach a badge to my black Figlio della Lupa shirt. It read: "Dio stramale-dica gli Inglesi" ("Goddamn the British"), and with a determined and energetic gesture, my mother tossed it right out the window. A self-confident woman, she was also very reserved, even keeping her love for us to herself. She never let herself go with excessive or exaggerated affection. But I remember that all it took was one gesture from her to make us feel safe.

Those were the days of the Fascist *colonie* (children's summer camps) along the coastline of the Adriatic Sea. Mother had been promoted to vice director of one at Misano Mare. My mother, my brother, and I took a train with shiny wooden seats and it stopped right in the middle of the countryside, as there was no station. The summer camp building, rising up white against the blue of the sky and the water, was as beautiful as a postcard. There are pictures of my mother and me on the beach. She would often wear a black wool bathing suit with white buttons that I really liked. I can still smell the walnut oil she would rub on our skin so we wouldn't get sunburned. We also went out on the water in what was known back then as a *moscone*, later called a *pattino*: a pedal boat made of two white-painted planks and a makeshift seat, the two oars in my mother's strong hands. I was afraid of the water. Today, that same fear has turned into a prudent and reasonable respect for it.

My mother was a very attractive woman and I was sure that her young assistants were rather infatuated with her. Sometimes I suffered because of it, especially when I found myself in

GIORGIO ARMANI WITH HIS MOTHER AND HIS BROTHER,
SERGIO, ON THE BEACH AT MISANO ADRIATICO, 1937

the dormitory, where the smell of boiled rice and peas wafted up from the kitchen. There's a beautiful large photograph of my mother, a close-up of her face, that I have always admired. To get it taken, I had to convince her to wear makeup, something she never would have normally done. But I wanted her to look like a movie star in one of those films where everything was perfect; I wanted this to be due to makeup that was applied properly, with just the right lighting and a beautiful dress. But my mother was beautiful even without makeup!

Then the war came directly to us, and it changed our lives. It certainly wasn't the war portrayed in the Luce films, in which multitudes praised the regime and bore witness to its incredible successes. We went from the peacefulness of that seaside camp to the fear of a bombed-out city. The cellars were our shelters. They were often just rooms made a little safer by propping up the ceilings with wooden poles. Every night we would all meet there. I was only eight yet I had to grow up quickly. During the war my mother got food for us that was far better than the kind you could buy with a ration card. Typically, the bread was like a stiff, flavorless tube that smelled of nothing and contained sticky dough inside—there's no other way to describe it. In the evening all we had to eat was milk with some coffee in it. Meat was out of the question. Sometimes we'd have some chicken, thanks to the generosity of family friends living in the countryside. That's where we would go at night because there was no danger of air raids. We'd return to the city on our bikes, when it was still dark and we were half-asleep. My mother would often pretend she was pregnant, hiding food under the roomy skirts women wore back then. This way the German patrols scouring the countryside wouldn't stop her from getting together a few eggs, a chicken, and two loaves of bread.

Sergio was tall and slim, and he always represented the ideal man for me. With his looks, his beautiful mouth and nose, his earnest blue eyes, he looked like the American movie star Joseph Cotten.

Rosanna, always with the two of us, had to put up with our innocent pranks. I think she always knew she would have to make her life her own. Of the three of us, she became the "independent" one, the sort of independence that still sets her apart today. She was a gorgeous child and she grew up to be a very attractive woman. Whenever I asked her if she would go out with my high school friends, she said no. She wasn't familiar with the world, and she didn't even seem interested in it—she was still wearing white bobby socks and men's shoes, black ones. Then she got into traveling around the world and it was hard to keep up with her. She traveled for work, but also because she was curious about nature and distant places; she was ahead of her time. Over the years, she was also a witness to many of the events in my life, and this has only served to strengthen the connection between us, without ever talking too much about it. But going back to the war, there were a few very near tragedies. Once we narrowly escaped being crushed when part of the house we were living in collapsed. Two people died—a brother and a sister, friends of ours. It was the first real shock of my life. Some time later, with Rosanna, I happened to be walking down the broad tree-lined street that led to the town's train station, where the evacuees were being sheltered. It was an important target for the air raids, and that day I suddenly became aware of the shadow of a military plane right behind us. I had just enough time to lunge into a ditch along the road and cover Rosanna with my green fustian jacket when the plane started shooting everywhere at random. It was at that moment, with bullets strewn along the road, I realized just how different viewing propaganda films was to witnessing a frightening reality.

But my memories of war are not only sad. One day, as we were getting back from the countryside, we crossed the River Trebbia at dawn on a makeshift boat steered by a ferryman, whose silhouette in the darkness was all I could make out. The dawn was pink and gray. The water was still. The small boat glided silently by a bridge that had fallen into disuse, and the German guards on the bridge didn't see us. This image is one of the most beautiful I can remember—paradoxical because it was in the middle of war—and one of the most unforgettable. We were drifting along a river in the Po Valley but as if we were immersed in a Japanese painting, a surreal and magical one.

In April 1945, the war ended for us. The lights on the streets, the houses, and the churches were lit up again and we could hear the murmuring of people on their balconies, at the windows, in the piazzas. And that was when we saw the Allied forces first march past. Some of them were Indians wearing large white turbans, while others were African-American soldiers. It was a world that until then we had only seen at the movies. We felt as though we had been reborn: it was the end of the airplanes, bombs, devastated cities. Of course, our own ruined city reflected the instability of this world that was just starting to emerge from the drama of war. Yes, the war was over, but we still had to survive what followed. My father paid the consequences for having worked for the Regime and my brother was forced into hiding for a period of time.

Another important event in my family's life took place a few days after the end of the war had been declared, while my sister Rosanna and I were walking past a movie theater close to our house. Once again, cinema played an integral role in my life because my sister's sudden move to look at the posters outside the theater saved her from the explosion that struck me a few yards away. A package of black gunpowder, left over from the war and easy to find in the empty barracks, had exploded; a few young friends had been blowing it up for fun. Seven people ended up in the hospital, including me. I spent twenty days there with my face swollen and my hair burnt away—it had been straight but grew back wavy—not knowing whether, once the bandaging was removed, I would ever be able to see again. But after a few days I noticed the sun filtering in through the window curtains: I would see again.

In the late 1940s, we moved from Piacenza to Milan. I arrived in Milan after attending a not particularly successful first year at a *liceo scientifico*, a secondary school that emphasizes the importance of the sciences. (The indulgence of a kind-hearted teacher, whom I will always be grateful to, kept me from having to take that year's final exams over again.) I was filled with the desire to do things, but I didn't know which direction to take. Milan didn't seem so welcoming at first, accustomed as I was to life in the province where everything was easy, within reach. But my parents had to choose, for economic reasons, to find a house on the outskirts. So everything was made to measure where we lived—ideal for someone who hailed from the Piacentina province. Gradually, I discovered that there was another Milan, with movie theaters that screened all the latest films and theaters I would attend with my father; a Milan where I rode my bike with my friends from school and where I spent the weekends taking pictures. At the Teatro alla Scala, the rivalry between "la Callas" and "la Tebaldi" came to life for us. We looked forward to movies with Sophia Loren, Silvana Mangano, and Gina Lollobrigida, and there were Italian Neorealist films that reminded us of Italy's war-torn past. I was deeply influenced by the images of those movies, somehow conditioned by them. Rosi, Bertolucci, Pasolini, Rossellini were to some degree responsible for this.

I found it hard to study, perhaps because I had too many distractions and perhaps also because I wasn't sure I had chosen the right kind of school. (A *liceo classico* would no doubt have kept me more focused on the books.) Everything around me made me feel restless, somehow dissatisfied with everything. People used to describe me as "the one who's always unhappy and unhappy with everyone." Fashion played no part, at least no apparent one at this point in my life. There seemed to be no trace of the spark of inspiration or sacred muse that most creative people recall when asked to talk about how they got started. At the time I had no connection at all to fashion—I never even breathed in the air of an atelier.

The first movie I remember seeing when I was a child was the epic *La corona di ferro* by Alessandro Blasetti. Made in 1941, it starred Massimo Girotti, Gino Cervi, Elisa Cegani, and the most famous couple in cinema back then, Luisa Ferida and Osvaldo Valenti, who play two characters, both beautiful and damned, who end up being murdered by the partisans—the same partisans whom I had often seen arrogantly parade through the streets of my city.

But, in our house, soccer and cinema were rivals: on Sundays, when my father listened to the game on the radio, we were expected to listen to it with him. We often went to the movies afterward. Our father would keep us on tenterhooks after the game, sitting at the table reading the newspaper, pretending nothing was going on. Then Sergio, who was great at drawing comics, would draw an imaginary movie house on a sheet of paper with all the seats occupied except two—ours. The sheet would be slipped under my father's eyes who, at that point, with a smile on his face, would give us permission to go, handing us the four lire we needed to be able to see a film like *The Adventures of Baron Munchausen*, the first color movie we saw.

My relationship with the movies has always been very strong, eventually even marking the various stages in my career in fashion. But when I was young, movies were my real education. Much more than what I learned at school, they shaped my imagination, my culture, and my tastes. A repertoire of aesthetic and narrative visions that inspire me and keep me up to date. The cinema was my escape from reality when I was young; my dreams came true right there in the theater. One particular event in my youth is linked to the cinema: my first plane trip. Although Rosanna was a very shy person, she had been chosen as the cover girl for a very famous popular magazine at the time, and so she got a call from Dino Risi, who was making the sequel to *Poveri ma belli*, to do a screen test. The year was 1958. They paid for our plane trip from Milan to Rome and, oddly enough, there was no one else in the cabin. The stewardess was very kind and took good care of us. We were incredibly excited.

When we arrived in Rome, waiting for us were the typical kinds of rascals that hung around movie people in Rome back then; they had been told to go pick up those two naïve Armani kids. First, they took us to Via Veneto, the heart of the "Dolce Vita," to let us soak up the atmosphere of cinematic Rome (although it was pouring rain and Via Veneto was practically deserted). Then they took us to Cinecittà to meet Dino Risi.

He was looking for a young Roman woman who would speak dialect while hanging clothes out on a balcony. The idea of Rosanna, a reserved and elegant young lady from Milan, playing the part seemed rather far-fetched to me.

I wasn't allowed to watch the screen test so, as I waited, I began wandering around the studios. At one point I walked by accident into Anna Magnani's dressing room, where she was being made up for Renato Castellani's *Nella città l'inferno*. I couldn't help saying hello to her, to which—although somewhat taken aback and looking at me inquisitively—she replied: "Well, good morning!" Then I found myself in a fake prison made of a long corridor with lots of cells. I saw a small woman coming from the other end; she was wearing a bathrobe with a tiny floral print and she had an unassuming, almost desolate air, a cigarette dangling from her lips. It was Giulietta Masina and I have always preferred to think that at that moment she was already playing the part of the prisoner. I didn't dare say hello to her.

As I had expected, they didn't choose Rosanna, but later, in 1960, she got her revenge by playing a small part in a scene in *Rocco e i suoi fratelli* by Luchino Visconti. Her role again had to do with doing household chores: she was supposed to iron a shirt and hand it to a character who I seem to remember was played by Renato Salvatori. Rosanna's career in cinema stopped there, while her work as a fashion model continued. At the age of seventeen she won a competition by the magazine *Arianna*, which launched new faces. She became a famous person and

PORTRAIT OF ROSANNA ARMANI, 1978

began living like one. Rosanna is not just a beautiful woman. I have always been fascinated by the fact that she lived her loves, her sadness, and her pain in a wholly independent way. After working as a fashion model and reporter, for twenty-two years she has worked steadily by my side. Owing to her strong personality, there were times when we have argued, but thanks to our mutual love and respect, we always succeed in resolving any issues with a laugh and completely in agreement. Rosanna's life is filled with the same things I like to cultivate: friendships with intelligent people, the ambience of other regions, travel. There is nothing banal about her or about what she does; she is gifted with a strong aesthetic sense and a keen, critical eye. For years, she worked closely with me as art director for the advertising campaigns and the publications of the *Emporio Armani Magazine*. Her relatively removed perspective of the fashion world and all that revolves around it has proved invaluable.

But the trait that perhaps best defines Rosanna is her scathing ironic wit. She is one of the people who has made me laugh the most, with her sharp insights and her great skill at imitating just about anyone's gestures, attitudes, and thoughts. (Exactly the way my mother knew how to.)

She also has a marvelous ability to fill the void. If she's not present, you miss her. Rosanna brings places to life; she creates ambience. She knows how to choose between what's worthwhile and what isn't. When Rosanna's around, there's laughter. It would have been unthinkable not to have had Rosanna by my side during my first encounter with Yves Saint Laurent, at his stunning home in Marrakech. We arrived there in a run-down van, wearing Bermuda shorts and T-shirts, which made us feel terribly uncomfortable before this man, who came to the door in a pinstriped double-breasted jacket and holding a small dog in his arms. But Rosanna always knew how to break the ice, and Yves Saint Laurent had an extremely kind and elegant manner about him. He invited us to sit on high-backed chairs made of leather and scented wood that had originally belonged to who knows which Far Eastern queens. We didn't talk about fashion. We talked about what the outside of his marvelous Majorelle garden risked becoming due to new constructions projects that weren't exactly in Moroccan style. When we said good-bye it was as if we had always known each other. He handed my sister his dog so that he could embrace me. He probably didn't know then that my future style would be drawn, in part, from his wonderful designs.

After attending the Liceo Scientifico Lorenzo Respighi in Piacenza for the first year, I did the last four years of high school in Milan, at the Leonardo da Vinci on Via Lulli. It was 1949 when we left Piacenza, and the experiences with my family up until then influenced my personality, which was already quite reserved. I sometimes think that I never really had a childhood or adolescence. I kept life at a skeptical distance as a sort of defense mechanism. Even many years later, a collaborator dared ask Sergio Galeotti, my partner, why I always looked so sad, despite all my success. Her question hit me hard. Today I interpret it as a sort of discomfort in expressing my feelings. It is a very accentuated form of shyness. This is why my words can at times seem somewhat callous or gruff. But it's all due to a rather painful self-consciousness. With my nieces and nephews, for instance, I've never been the uncle to play with; instead, I've become a father figure to them. Just as I feel like a "father" to many of my collaborators, both near and far, scattered around the world.

Among other subjects, I studied French, and I can still remember my teacher, who looked exactly like Giuseppe Verdi. I thought it was very cruel of him to read the grades out loud as he sat at his desk, and, whenever he got to my name, I can remember him saying: "I see that Armani has improved, zero plus!" Each time was a huge blow to my self-esteem. I never understood why he did it. Perhaps he thought I was a loafer, or perhaps he thought I wasn't capable of learning that marvelous language. However, by the end of those four years I *had* learned French. Finally, it was time to take the fifth-year exam. I was the last one on the list. It was a beautiful day in late July; the sky was cloudless. I was daydreaming, looking out the window at the airplanes headed to exotic places. I felt a growing desire to escape. I don't know whether the teacher was aware of how I was feeling, but as if to help me out he asked: "Talk to us about the winds." And I said, hesitatingly: "The winds are those things that . . ." but I didn't even have time to explain. All the teacher said was: "Thank you, Armani. See you again in September."

I WANTED TO BE A DOCTOR AND
BECAME A FASHION DESIGNER INSTEAD

I had always wanted to be a doctor, ever since I was a child. A.J. Cronin's books about being a country doctor had made a deep impression on me: I loved the idea of a person who saved the lives of the elderly and the young alike. However, when I got to university I soon realized that I didn't have the focus that was needed to study such a demanding subject. I lasted just two years, also discovering just how precarious the Italian university system was back then.

As a student who was *fuori corso*, meaning that I could study at the university even though I had fallen behind with my exam schedule, I could no longer put off doing compulsory military service. So I quit medicine without too many regrets, also because I had been rather disappointed, but mostly because I wanted to help out my family and contribute in my own way.

GIORGIO ARMANI DURING HIS MILITARY SERVICE, 1956

I left home to do my military service in 1955. At the time, I was just one of the many unsophisticated twenty-year-olds whose nights and weekends consisted of putting on a record at a friend's house, drinking a bottle of whiskey just to feel like some hotshot. But the time had come to give up this rather unexciting, albeit reassuringly predictable, lifestyle, and military service seemed to be a sensible way to move on with my life.

I took a small wardrobe for all occasions with me—including a tennis racquet, which, needless to say, when I arrived at the Centro Addestramento Reclute (CAR) in Siena, they kindly suggested I send back home. They said a uniform would be more than enough of a wardrobe, and there would be no tennis courts for the recruits. I realized how hard the service was going to be from the very first meal they served us: pasta and meat mixed all together in a metal tray, spiced up with a cockroach. But one day, after some time had passed, I looked at myself in the mirror and saw a grown man who reminded me of a young American soldier, tanned from being out in the sun of the Sienese hills, and with a certain satisfied air, even without his tennis racquet. After my training period I was sent to Riva del Garda, a place that is delightful in summer but rather melancholy in winter. I arrived there on a winter's day. I had to put up with the kinds of physical discomfort that I wasn't at all accustomed to. The alarm went off at six a.m. after a night spent on a cot covered in a coarse sheet (which, by the time the whole experience had ended, had begun to feel quite comfortable to me). The relentless marching would finally end with all of us sitting together in our sweaty, dusty uniforms in a cramped, smelly classroom where we were taught our lessons on military theory. But what struck me most, perhaps, was that every single evening we had to wait until after nine p.m. to gain access to the dorms, a length of time that can seem interminable when you're crouched outside the door half-asleep and filled with nostalgia for home.

Undoubtedly, my training at the CAR had a positive effect on shaping my character. I discovered that kindness, not arrogance, would get me further, and that being polite, such as by saying: "Would you please pass me the oil," at the table, actually impressed people. As I had studied medicine for two years, the captain physician felt authorized to assign me to the infirmary, where my activity consisted in giving routine shots and handing out pills when required. I kept loneliness at bay by painting pictures, which have since been lost. I was glad for my medical studies and my newfound discipline when, having been given permission to go to Milan for a bonus vacation, I returned to find forty soldiers in the dorm sick with Asian flu. From Riva del Garda I was sent to the military hospital at Verona. I appreciated its peaceful, orderly atmosphere, the rituals, the regular pace, the nuns that "flew" in and out of the rooms and who had their favorites. Luckily, I was one of them. It was actually because of the attentions of an elderly nun named Lancisia that I was able to return to Milan nine months earlier than planned.

When I returned to Milan, although I stood by my decision not to continue my university studies, I still didn't have a clue what I wanted to do. With no profession, I felt as though I was lagging behind everyone. A friend suggested I try getting a job at the high-end department store La Rinascente, and she gave my name to the person in charge of the advertising department. They needed a catalogue and quite brazenly I convinced them I could produce one. I had never gone to an art school or a photography school, and when Rosanna and I went to see the woman in charge of the project, a woman with a snide manner who was very sure of herself, I showed her the photographs that as an amateur I had taken of my sister—photographs that had neither technique nor inspiration. They were tossed out, of course, but I ended up working with Signorina Ada for three whole years (although my boss seemed more interested in going out to get coffee than in the future of her assistant!).

My first job was to assist the various architecture studios that installed the exhibitions, as well as organize the window dressing, but neither of these tasks particularly required any creativity. My first truly professional job was working with the menswear buyers, helping them to choose the products to be put on sale. I soon came up against their deep-rooted habits: these were buyers who were accustomed to buying the same products, year after year, and now they were being questioned by a young man without much experience. It was a long training period that no doubt greatly influenced my continuing to work in fashion. I could have kept on doing the same job for the rest of my life. But hanging over my head like the proverbial sword of Damocles were the words my boss used to reproach me one day: "Armani, you'll always be a good 'second.'" It was my umpteenth encounter with a certain woman that prompted me to choose another profession, this one for life. I would often see this woman in the halls, and even from a distance I could smell her intense, unforgettable perfume. I would watch her sashay by in a wild mink fur with horizontal stripes. She was the personification of beauty, but she was also the subject of much gossip. Michelangelo Antonioni had actually asked her to take a screen test for the movie *Cronaca di un amore*, although he later chose Lucia Bosé, another movie icon I have always loved. Her friend Nino Cerruti, the owner of Hitman, a company of fine fabrics and menswear, was looking for someone to fill a position that was not so common in Italy, although it had already existed in France: a *stilista*, a fashion designer.

So I started working with "Signor Nino." That was 1965. Working at Hitman, I finally became a part of fashion. My job was to create a new image for men. Despite the fact that he could exploit both advanced technology and the many Italian-American experts who worked for his company, Cerruti asked me to find some new solutions to make a man's suit less rigid and more comfortable, less industrial and more sartorial. By "deconstructing" the jacket, I made it come alive on the body, using fabrics that weren't at all traditional. It was no doubt Nino Cerruti's farsightedness that allowed me to move about in that environment, where it was easy to come across fixed and static systems. Meanwhile, as I was saying, in France, fashion was moving at a very fast pace, making good use of its avant-garde recruits, first among them being Pierre Cardin, the inventor of the designer label. There were Valentino, Saint Laurent, Kenzo, Rabanne, Emmanuelle Khanh, Karl Lagerfeld, and many others who worked in women's fashion in particular. So I was especially proud when Nino Cerruti introduced some men's styles into the womenswear collection he was presenting in Paris, in his new boutique on Rue Royale.

By then the fashion scene had become filled with people who were inventive and curious. There was a great ferment underway that mixed everything together. Suggestions and ideas came from everywhere, opportunities that had to be taken at once. Being a stylist proved to be a job that lay somewhere between the wildest imagination and the greatest practicality. Almost like a politician, one had to both follow and guide, observe and anticipate. Fashion stylists had to be able to create trends, suggest, even moving people's desires and dreams farther forward. I was beginning to feel that menswear was too limited, and that's when I began, with Cerruti's tacit approval, to design women's fashions for other companies. This turned out to be a wonderful sort of apprenticeship, as it gave me the chance to deal with everything from prêt-à-porter to accessories, from leather to knitwear.

At the time, Palazzo Pitti was the headquarters of the fashion show. At first anonymously, and then, having ended my collaboration with the Cerruti group, giving the collections my own name, I, too, became a member of the new ranks of Italian fashion. There's a picture from 1966 that I'm very fond of, which shows me lying on a sun lounger on the beach in Forte dei Marmi. I was not a habitué, but I had been invited to spend a weekend, and there I met two people who left their mark on me. The first of these was a very attractive woman who was also extremely sensitive and romantic, as well as being self-assured. I saw her sometime later by coincidence on a boat next to mine, and then many years after that. On the latter occasion she said to me: "We were very beautiful, Giorgio." Perhaps she thought I hadn't recognized her.

The other person I met that weekend, quite by chance just two days later, was Sergio Galeotti. Two separate events, but incredibly related. I met Sergio at the end of a day at the beach, in the famous nightclub called La Capannina. He was dressed simply, and he was very charming, a good Tuscan from Pietrasanta. He possessed both the verve and nonchalance typical of twenty-year-olds. The more I spoke to him about my experiences, the goals I had achieved as well as my aspirations, the more he understood my potential. He lived in Versilia and yet wanted to move to Milan to test himself, but above all to experience this adventure together with me. I got busy looking for a job for him, and found him one as a draftsman in the prestigious architectural practice, Peressutti and Rogers. Sergio became a part of my world and, at the same time, a part of the city of Milan that was changing. We lived in an apartment on Viale Lazio that I felt was a beautiful part of Milan with lots of trees, where I could take my dog Jago out for a run. The interior of the house was decorated in gray and beige tones, of course, with carpeting that matched the sofa and the cushions (in true 1970s style). There were kenzia plants arranged in the middle of the apartment, the unconscious foreshadowing of the exoticism that was to become a must in my collections. And on a more frivolous note, there were ostrich feathers in every shade of mauve in one corner, which I had purchased at Biba's on Carnaby Street in London.

It was in that house that Sergio and I discussed working together for the first time. We were waiting for my first design studio to be finished: three rooms on Corso Venezia. One large room with imitation Japanese-lacquer tables, actually laminated plastic edged with brass, was set up as a showroom. The second room was for Sergio, who managed our business, with a secretary who took care of whatever needed to be done, and whom we had clearly told: "You should keep studying in the meantime, you never know what might happen!" The third room was for shipments, administration, and logistics.

At first, our work consisted of style consulting, while I was the one responsible for the fashion shows. Soon the money started coming in. Sergio learned to be the manager that, perhaps, he had never really wanted to be. I think he loved life too much to really love that job, and all the work he had to do because of our success was overwhelming and endless. Although he turned out to be quite skillful in business and have bold insights, sometimes he would talk to me about his discontentment—my work was creative and in many ways fun, while his most certainly was not, as he was forced to act "tough" in his relations with the business world. To be honest, I feel I didn't pay enough attention to his concerns, something that still bothers me today. Once when we had a difference of opinions, I laid into him, saying: "This is how it has to be done," to which he replied, "Sorry, sorry, sorry." It was a tone of voice that I had never heard before, resentful as well as a little sad. Nevertheless he protected me from everybody, from the whole world really. That was Sergio.

Everyone appreciated Sergio's great personality, his friends obviously did, but so did the press. His warm manner was the exact opposite of my aloofness. But Sergio was also quite unpredictable. Just for the sake of surprising me—at least, that's what he said—one day he pretended he was leaving to go to Pietrasanta, which he sometimes did on the weekends so that he could visit his mother who lived there. After a few hours, without warning, I heard a voice calling me. It was his voice, but I had no idea where it was coming from. I was confused and, rather petulantly, called out: "Sergio, where are you?" That's when he jumped out of a closet, shouting: "I fooled you!" On another occasion he was in the bathroom for what seemed

FOLLOWING PAGES: PORTRAIT OF GIORGIO ARMANI, 1970,
SERGIO GALEOTTI, *L'UOMO VOGUE*, 1982

like forever. So I went to the door and shouted: "Come on, Sergio, open up!" I pushed the door open and there he was lying in the tub, completely under water, his eyes open, staring straight at the ceiling. We had recently seen the movie *Les Diaboliques* and it had made an impression on both of us. Another time he spread toothpaste all over his face and then walked zombie-like over to the door to my studio. Get the picture?

Sergio certainly wasn't compliant. He was quite the opposite: bold and brave, maybe a bit too reckless. Like the time we gave an interview to a reporter who wanted information about the endorsements at our shows. The condition was that we wouldn't talk about money. Naturally, the first question was about how much money Giorgio Armani had offered. Sergio grabbed the reporter's handbag, which was on the desk, and threw it at our impolite guest.

There was complete agreement between us in all things. But maybe I was the one calling the shots, because in my life there has never been love that hasn't turned into something long-lasting, into deep understanding and total friendship. This has always been my way of loving.

It was the early 1970s. We had bushy salt-and-pepper sideburns and could afford our first exotic vacation. We chose Corfu, driving there in our famous white VW. The whole time it felt as though we were walking on air. We had just moved our headquarters to Via Durini, where we had made our first big investment: Palazzo Durini, a vast and prestigious eighteenth-century abode whose ceilings were decorated with the original frescoes, with huge spaces. We felt we had taken an important step. The media followed our move with great interest and we thought we would throw a big housewarming party for Christmas that year. I remember the decor: an endless number of pillows in gold fabric and candlelit pineapple trophies. Those who were there still remember what a great success it was. At our headquarters on Via Durini, our business grew quickly, with the first acknowledgments from the rest of the world flowing in.

America had discovered me, and in the late 1970s we founded the Giorgio Armani Corporation, which we needed to do to be able to deal with the American market. American women were the first to appreciate my work—and my audacity. In those days, fashion was filled with pervasive, exaggerated, eccentric trends that were much to the liking of the avant-garde media. Going against the grain, I chose to subtract instead of add, to react against style that as a banner of creativity served as an end in itself, rather than being for the benefit of the consumer. Of course, I was also a victim of those trends. I, too, wore clothing like a mauve velvet or floral-print jacket—and later regretted it. But it was also part of the evolution of fashion. Trying out new things was essential to my work. Our collections were manufactured by the same producers for whom I designed the clothes that bore their labels. The success of the system was based on this circulation of ideas. My partnership with the Gruppo Finanziario Tessile (GFT) was a crucial part of that.

Marco Rivetti, the chairman of GFT, who had a profound impact on the global distribution of Italian labels, just as Nino Cerruti had on the menswear sector, became our partner for the women's collections, a mutually agreeable arrangement—in fact, even the media looked favorably on it. I felt the need to have a solid producer who was willing to invest in a new name, and Marco, in turn, wanted to enhance the group's reputation with up-to-date collections that took into account changing contemporary lifestyles.

Those were wonderful years, during which I was busy with collections that combined tradition and the innovation that women had been yearning for. It was during this time that the picture of me with Sergio in our studio was taken, right in the middle of a discussion about the latest collections with GFT. The particular collection, inspired by the Japanese painter Utamaro and samurai costumes, were masterpieces of technique and dressmaking. We exhibited the collection in Palazzo Durini, on three separate walkways around which the public, seated close-up, could admire the uniqueness of the pieces. While the collection wasn't particularly successful from a commercial point of view, it resonated, and is still resonating today. Marco's confidence in our work was in no way diminished. He seemed fully aware that this was a carefully studied, perfectly timed *coup de théâtre*. Sergio's satisfied grin in the picture is further proof of that.

I had worked in menswear for many years, exploring alternative ways to clothe men, always seeking a sort of elegance that would never become arrogance. I began to perceive the advance of a new kind of femininity that required a wardrobe that would fully complement the way men dressed. I felt that the two sexes, even in fashion, needed to meet on an equal level. Feminism, so explosive in those years when I was getting started, undoubtedly influenced my way of thinking about fashion. I have great esteem for women—I think they know how to be seductive without resorting to an exhibitionism that easily slips into vulgarity and excess.

I have always been convinced that an outfit can help women to make choices that will determine the outcome of a meeting, that will rule out what is useless or wrong. I have above all tried to offer a way of dressing that is coherent with this unprecedented kind of femininity that forced men to look at women with new eyes. My purpose in fashion is to offer a less severe, less rigid allure to the male figure, and a less mannered style to the female figure—all the while preserving elegance and distinction and the idea that others should notice you for your mind and your self-esteem. I imagined women in new roles, women who would no longer have to pull their skirts down over their knees when they sat down or unbutton their tight jackets as soon as they took their places at the table for a business meeting. The elegance of the gesture, for me, has always been crucial; it is an integral part of style and one's way of dressing.

With this ideal paramount, I believed that a jacket can portray what a person is like much more than exposing the body.

There's no need to take your clothes off to reveal yourself: all you need is a soft, unstructured blazer that falls naturally from shoulders that aren't constrained, that are free from reinforcements and yet are perfect all the same. What could be sexier than a skintight jacket that wraps the wearer's body naturally and conveys his or her sensuality?

Sergio and I became convinced that it was time to found a new fashion brand with my name. I was the creative and he was the manager. I can't really remember when the emotional debut happened, because everything took place in such quick succession that it has become a single episode, with salient moments that seem as if they happened yesterday. But I know that over the past forty years all I've had time for is work. I've never had any other pastimes. I am engaged in an obsessive relationship with my work, perhaps, as I've been accused of, with almost maniacal perfectionism that is trying to control everything. You might ask why I didn't delegate the work. The answer is that the more creative a job, the harder it is to explain to another person what you want, often because quite often you yourself don't know.

As head of a company I know that any delegating, which has always concerned the development strategy, must involve the right person. It's a complicated mechanism, made up of trust and supervision, of a perfect balance between esteem and caution. In time, I learned to be more mindful of every-thing, and I even learned not to demand others come up with brilliant ideas. Ultimately, the choices have always been mine, and often my idea is the winning one.

We had just signed into existence Giorgio Armani SpA with a fully paid-up stock of ten million lire. The company was located in the offices of Corso Venezia; the number of staff members had grown and everyone did a bit of everything: the CEO would seal the cardboard boxes containing the clothing to be shipped, the assistant designer operated the copy machine, the secretary took down the orders. Sergio and I would do whatever needed to be done, in the most wonderful atmosphere of collaboration that I can remember. There we presented the first Giorgio Armani menswear collection: suits made of all-natural fabrics, linen that was made softer by using unconventional treatments so that it draped nicely, jackets that were less structured, trousers that were roomy and flowing. The point was to give those who wore our styles an air that was deliberately between "scruffy" and "sophisticated." The fashion show, albeit short, not only drew the interest of the press, but also of a small but important group of innovators, artists, and intellectuals who appreciated that look, which reminded them of their own jackets hanging in their closets at home.

Business started taking off. In 1976 the turnover was 569 million lire (a little over two million dollars today), which seemed like a huge amount as we'd started out at zero the year before. Our first years in fashion were also dark and difficult years for Italy.

GIORGIO ARMANI IN HIS STUDIO ON VIA BORGONUOVO IN MILAN
WITH A PAINTING BY SILVIO PASOTTI IN THE BACKGROUND, 1978

All you had to do was look out the windows of our offices to feel the tension on the streets. There was a spirit of protest, a violent questioning of every convention. It seemed as though nothing could be saved of what had been deemed "normal": relationships and social customs, rules, and even taste.

Having to wipe out the past forced us to start from scratch, to come to terms with this new world and to distinguish what needed to be preserved. In those years it was as if through fashion we tried to capture the best side of that revolution and carry it over into an era when elegance would inevitably be different.

Terrible news of bombs, clashes, and shootings disturbed me, but I tried to remain psychologically detached, to move forward, pushing aside the idea that what I was doing might no longer be worthwhile. We were just beginning to be successful. I couldn't overlook what was going on outside, but I couldn't allow it to affect our work or to influence it negatively.

At Corso Venezia, in my red lacquer studio, I spent a lot of time drawing, seeking my identity in the pencil line. Saint Laurent's maquettes were one inspiration; their example helped me to achieve a softer but also more androgynous image. Another inspiration was the way in which Coco Chanel had successfully matched small lightweight jackets, decorated with her legendary camellia, with trousers that were cut like a man's, without foregoing charm and femininity.

Everything happened during the same year—the news of Sergio's illness, his immediate hospitalization, the helplessness, the courage, on my part as well, to insist on talking about the future, as if nothing were wrong. I felt desperately incapable of protecting him. And the words he said to me in Paris, after seeing a film of the latest collection, will forever be in my heart: "You're rich, handsome, and young, and look what's happened to you." It was as if he were describing my pain, as if he had forgotten that he was the one who was dying.

In the meantime, I continued to deal with the collections, missing his reassuring presence. On the phone one day, while he was at his country home near Paris, he asked me where I would be going in August. It was a blow straight to the heart. August was always the month we left together for our well-deserved holiday—how could he possibly think I was going to leave him alone, even though he had his family around him? He died in August. Our company had just celebrated its tenth anniversary. During that dreadful year, I lived as though I were holding my breath, without thinking about the inevitable, working day in and day out. And what came after was terribly difficult. Most people thought I wouldn't be able to make it, all except the people closest to me, like Leo Dell'Orco and my family. Many believed I would collapse psychologically and that the future of the Giorgio Armani company was uncertain. It would have been quite natural to let oneself go, to give up, which is what my management expected would happen and was ready for. I had even fooled myself into thinking that I could count on people who were above suspicion.

Leo especially was very close to me. I treasured his practicality and his clear-sightedness. We were never going to give up our work, which had been Sergio's work, too. Leo's real name is Pantaleo. He was born in Bisceglie and he has always kept close ties with the part of his family that has stayed in Puglia. When I met him—it was fate!—he was a draftsman in a large Italian industry that had nothing to do with fashion. We met outside where we both lived, on the few feet of greenery where our dogs became friends. Handsome Leo was very happy to join my work group, bringing with him his kindness, his shyness, his total devotion. We were in Corso Venezia and his activity was divided between menswear fashion shows and showrooms, supporting Sergio's work. Gifted with a certain sensitivity when it came to fashion, in time he was given jobs with greater responsibility, until he became the Leo that we all know and appreciate. Today, you might say he's my right-hand man. What I like most of all about his personality is the fact that he's always ready to smile at the first meeting of the morning. I will never forget how much he helped me through the sad events surrounding Sergio's illness, in that undisturbed countryside not far from Paris, where Sergio spent the final hours of his life. Leo is the person to whom I confided my most private, personal thoughts about work and other matters, thoughts he has kept confidential. (Thank you, Leo!)

When we showed in Rockefeller Center, our first New York event, I remember Leo on the catwalk wearing a black velvet

GIORGIO ARMANI AND LEO DELL'ORCO IN MILAN, RUNWAY SEASON
FINALE, GIORGIO ARMANI MEN, FALL/WINTER 2004–2005

tuxedo. It was an especially important evening for a young man who, from the draftsman's desk, had made it all the way to a Giorgio Armani fashion show in legendary New York City. From backstage we couldn't see the whole length of the catwalk. No video had been set up, which in those days was still very expensive. During the show, we couldn't see what was happening outside. All we could hear was a very surreal—and worrying—silence. With a huge, beautiful moon peering down on us after the last group came out, the men wearing black velvet tuxedoes and the women, including my niece Silvana, in black velvet one-piece outfits with huge calla lilies pinned to their shoulders, the silence seemed even more deafening. Sergio was standing in a corner behind me, almost hiding, on the verge of crying: a flop in New York would have been a severe setback. Then suddenly, as if by magic, someone came running to us, shouting: "A huge success! The audience is applauding wildly!" We just hadn't been able to hear them. We could start breathing again.

In the meantime, the first store that sold Giorgio Armani in Italy opened on Via del Babuino in Rome. It was a franchise run by a dear friend. Our own first boutique opened in Milan, combining the strategy of direct distribution, the multibrand, with the franchise. For years we continued with a pioneering spirit, driven by the collective will not to let one another down. Life is full of the unexpected. I remember how hard it was for me to accept that the big house in Broni, which we purchased after two days of searching in the Oltrepò Pavese, had been seen by Sergio only once. We discovered he was ill a week later. Sergio and I talked about how we would have liked to convert that beautiful villa into a house where we could spend our weekends. Surrounded by a park of centuries-old trees, it was like a dream, far from the city and from its frenetic pace. We imagined keeping ponies, deer, alpacas, and several pedigree dogs there, as well as farm animals that would naturally also mean a series of "intruders," predators like weasels and foxes. We dreamed of enjoying this place amid thirty-seven acres of land in the Oltrepò foothills the way one would a country home—barefoot and with the quiet rhythms and ambience that would be at one with our way of being.

I cannot forget to talk about Pantelleria, with its small stone houses called *dammusi*. It has taken me thirty years to transform it into an island within an island, creating memorable spots, like beautiful scenes: a palm grove with two hundred trees. A vineyard for the Passito, the grapes that grow on the island. The sea right in front of our house—blue and important. Sergio and I spent many of our vacations there over the years, vacations with our best friends and with our family. Thirty years of happiness. Something we couldn't have done without. Sergio was the one who wanted the house in Forte dei Marmi, just a few miles from where he was born. It was the first house that Sergio and I lived in together during our vacations in August and the last one he saw before leaving for America, where he went for treatment. Every corner of this house reminds me of the time I spent with him and his satisfaction at owning it. In this house I also spent the first part of the lockdown due to the pandemic. I lived that first moment of collective shock with the people dearest to me, Leo first and foremost, taking the opportunity to rethink many things, not only about my life, but about my business as well. We live on Planet Earth, which is unique and unrepeatable: we need to respect it in every way possible, and that is what I'm doing. I never felt alone in my house in Forte dei Marmi. During those months a special relationship developed with the people there that greatly impressed me. A letter I wrote to *WWD* led to a chain of marvelous reactions.

The house in Antigua in the Caribbean Sea was bought in response to a psychologically difficult period. I was convalescing after the illness that had struck me in 2009: that house on the rocks overlooking the small white beach helped me to survive a time of great uncertainty.

I heeded the words of the communications experts and my watchful public relations people: New York City had to be part of my world. I now have a penthouse at 91 Central Park West, in a prestigious historic building. It started out as a kind of official business headquarters, but it has become the home where I stay when I go to New York. One of my first visits to New York was with my family, including my dogs. Central Park was covered in snow. It was like being in a movie: we, from Piacenza, were in New York City—something completely different! But with them I am always Giorgio, never "Mr. Armani." It is the official world that makes me feel like Mr. Armani: the parties, the fashion shows, the events. Depending on which house I am residing in, I have always played a role in which I become an actor representing myself, alongside the nostalgia of my private life, the warmth of my homes, the trust of my friends and family. A house in the mountains was always my dream. In my younger days, my family would go to the mountains for our vacation. The sea was far from our horizon. In the mountains I would spend two weeks each year, often passing by the wooden chalets that evoked for me a sense of intimacy and warmth. So when I saw an eighteenth-century house in the Engadin Valley, with its huge barn, it was love at first sight. I just had to buy it. And it was during my illness that I—working from my hospital bed—and my collaborators developed the design for it. Inspired by a Japanese home I had seen in a wonderful interior decor magazine, this became quite a charming house, and one that was considered not at all in contrast with the Engadin surroundings. Attaching a lot of importance to the aesthetic factor in human relationships can be a flaw, but I'm afraid that that's the way I am, even though I'm quite aware that an elegant style can certainly hide the fact that there's nothing behind it. This aesthetic sensibility has always been the reason for my dissatisfaction at the reality around me. And in regard to my obsession with aesthetics, it is clear to me just how fruitful my collaboration with the photographer Aldo Fallai has been—an extremely successful relationship, albeit unpredictable, between a true Florentine and a Milanese by adoption. With Rosanna's graceful mediation, always supportive of both of us, Aldo created images that were exactly how I had imagined and wanted them to be.

If I think of all the images I have produced over time, it's hard to date them because I have always staged a "he" and a "she" of the so-called complicit couple, the Bonnie and Clyde of yesterday and today.

By the late 1980s I was a unique figure, an innovator, and the head of a company. I'd had to learn fast, but the situation at the company was becoming quite complex; decisions had to be made that couldn't wait for me to complete my "apprenticeship." In 1988, for example, I signed an important agreement with Luxottica, a major company specializing in eyeglasses, for the production of Armani eyewear. Also, in 1998, Giorgio Armani SpA had reached a consolidated turnover of 1.502 billion lire (equal to 774.6 million dollars) with net profits of 242 billion lire, while the overall value of Armani products sold in the world was almost 6 billion lire.

In Paris we had recently opened a large Emporio Armani, on Boulevard Saint-Germain. So we decided to organize a big fashion show, a one-off event. I was puzzled by the decision to set up a large tent at the Place Saint-Sulpice in the heart of Saint-Germain, as I doubted that the city would allow us to occupy that space for three whole days, but the authorization mysteriously arrived. Three hours before the show, however, the authorities sent an inspector to check the installation and they found that one of the walkways was narrower than it was legally supposed to be. In two hours we managed to solve the problem and waited for the authorities to send someone back to check again. But that never happened. So we had no authorization, and there were policemen all around the large structure with one thousand two hundred guests waiting to enter.

I made a couple of phone calls. The first of these was to an important Italian politician I had met by chance during a vacation in Pantelleria. I asked if he could do something about it. He answered: "My dear Armani, it's a matter of politics." The second call I made was to a very influential person in French fashion. I described the situation and he seemed to sympathize with me. He told me to call back in an hour, which I did, but the office was closed by then.

The fashion show was held all the same for the chosen few inside the structure. The story was in the newspapers and we made sure we had learned our lesson: this near fiasco helped us to get ready for the same fashion show in New York, which went on without a hitch. In February 2020 I had another show behind closed doors, but it was my decision to do so, which attracted lots of criticism. It was the beginning of the pandemic and I felt a moral duty to protect my team and my public. It was the right decision.

Way back in 1999, Gruppo Armani was already quite wealthy, independent, riding on the crest of the wave. But the end of the millennium was close at hand, and for me the year 2000 felt like a fateful date for the overall balance of my company and its future. We were bringing the century to a close with a yearly turnover of 1.680 billion lire (875.2 million dollars) and a net profit of 212.2 billion lire. These were important numbers. It's easy to see how proud we were of what we had built. Naturally, faced with many proposals—partnerships, special agreements, shareholder investments—some of my managers suggested that we make important changes at the top, essentially a new internal organization. My answer was always the same: the success of Giorgio Armani lies in the fact that the company depends on the choices of a single person helped by loyal collaborators. For me, the organization is like a physiological entity, not what the newspapers, to some extent heartlessly, call "the Armani legacy," a reality that I have been carrying on my shoulders for two decades. The choice might seem egocentric, removed from what's happening in the world, but new ways of thinking in fashion haven't always achieved satisfactory results.

I have my succession in mind and that is how it will be. Trustworthy Leo and Silvana are my lieutenants of style.

My niece Roberta has always been the little one in the family, the one who somehow needs to be protected. Even though she has always had the personality of someone who doesn't like to be told what to do. She went through some hard times with her father, who passed away, and she is capable of showing great tenderness. Every now and then, she simply sends me a message saying: "Uncle, I love you." Her job is to liaise with the members of the jet set, the VIPs. Thanks to her radiance, her beauty, and her generosity, she is quite successful at it. Everyone loves her. I think it's because everyone realizes that first of all she has to deal with me, which is in and of itself a difficult job! She accepts the star system yet never forgets the boundaries that we have agreed to and set for ourselves. She protects me without giving the impression that she does. It can't be an easy thing to do. And she's also very curious. An example of this is that she chooses the places where she goes on vacation without allowing the system, which can be quite foolish at times, to tell her where she *has* to go.

It's always wonderful when I see my niece Silvana coming to meet me, dressed impeccably, so perfect and personalized. Everything she does is elegant. She's affectionate and caring and, just like her sister Roberta, she defends and protects me. She began her profession as a fashion model representing the kind of woman who is close to my way of thinking, and then moved on to working more directly and responsibly in the actualization of the womenswear collections right by my side, always open to evaluating her own work, even to accepting my opinions if they go against her own. She loves the house and all that it represents. She loves her dogs.

GIORGIO ARMANI WITH HIS NEPHEW, ANDREA CAMERANA, AND LEO DELL'ORCO IN MARRAKECH, 1988

GIORGIO ARMANI WITH HIS NIECES
SILVANA AND ROBERTA, 1990S

She's liable to fall in love easily and she enthuses over things. She has a very sophisticated beauty, which is something I love about women.

Andrea is Rosanna's son, and he's a lot like her. I have always appreciated his sense of maturity, which, even though he is quite young, he expresses in his opinions, in the way he takes an interest in things. He's witty, with the same ability to judge things as his mother, and he firmly defends his private life and his choices. He has a family. Maria Vittoria and Margherita are his little girls. My caricature, in this book, was sketched by Maria Vittoria. It is with that drawing made a few years ago that I am pleased to end this first part of my story. I realize that the events I describe, so heartfelt and personal, take place one after another on these pages, often ignoring the chronology of their occurrence, even rewriting it at times; anticipating facts and then going back to them. My readers will forgive me: reliving your life in words is like swimming in a swollen river. The to and fro of the episodes is never-ending, and that is how I like to remember them. This is the sentimental Giorgio Armani, whom I often protect and rarely show, but whom I have wanted to reveal because now is the time to do so. From here on, instead, these pages will take another turn: an equally personal one, but more pragmatic, more rigorous. A rigorousness that hides the flame behind the iciness, becoming a sort of manual: my own manual, about life and work, for all to use.

GIORGIO ARMANI AS SEEN BY HIS THREE-YEAR-OLD
GREAT-NIECE, MARIA VITTORIA CAMERANA, 2010

GIORGIO ARMANI AS SEEN BY GARY

GIORGIO ARMANI AS SEEN BY FRANCESCO CLEMENTE, 1993

MY BYWORDS,
FOR EVERYONE TO USE

ME

Describing yourself is never easy, but it's an exercise that, when you reach the age of eighty, you can no longer put off. It helps you to set down some key points, to look at yourself in earnest, inwardly as well as outwardly. Even though I never stop trying to evolve and improve, I have reached the kind of wisdom that allows me to accept my merits and my faults in peace. Growing means adapting the perfect world of ideas to the imperfect world of reality. It takes a lifetime to do so, but you'll succeed in the end. For example, there's something I've learned over the years, which is to try to tone down my intransigence: I'm very tough on myself, even more so than on those around me, but I also understand more deeply now that to err is human. Simply put, I want the best: I aspire to perfection, and I do what it takes to achieve it. I admire discretion, and I loathe exhibitionism. I am drawn to silence, and I love the essentials; I dislike excess and noise, even when they're metaphorical. I trust only a few people, and I need the support of my family around me as well as their blood ties and bonds of affection that I have cultivated over the years.

GIORGIO ARMANI WITH HIS CAT ISOLINA, 1989

There are very few people who have really meant something to me, but when I believe in a relationship, I give it my all, no holds barred. Whether it's my sister, my nieces and nephews, my closest collaborators, the people I love, it makes no difference. In others, I admire entrepreneurship, devotion, commitment, and creativity. In others, laziness, negligence, and sloppiness irk me and make me highly critical; the principles my parents taught me and my upbringing have shown me that to be successful you need to work, and that is why I truly believe that idleness is the mother of all vice. I'm a man who gets things done, not one who just talks about them—a man of action, not of celebration or, worse still, self-celebration. Often, I don't care to discuss such things with my collaborators or with the outside world. It may be because of my excessive sense of discretion, which stems from my austere middle-class sense of morality, but it's hard for me to show my private side, which I guard jealously. I detest the idea of flattering myself or resting on my laurels as I contemplate my successes. These are undoubtedly many, but there could be far more. Each success is a point of departure for a new challenge. Challenges: I love them more than anything else, and not so much out of a hunger for fame, or because they lead to more income, but because they allow me to know how the world is evolving while keeping me young. Youth is lost when you stop being in harmony with the times. I have built my empire upon the observation of everyday reality. From the very beginning of my career, I rejected the outmoded figure of the fashion designer locked inside his or her ivory tower thinking up amazing clothing for privileged women. I wanted to clothe real women and real men, and then, as time passed, the equally real young people of Emporio Armani. I wanted my outfits to spark their awareness of the fact that they are the protagonists of a fast-moving society. Creating fashion does not just mean creating clothes—fashion is also a workshop in which attitudes are experimented with and new perspectives adapted. I keep my eyes trained on what lies ahead of me, on the horizon, because it is only by keeping a wide perspective and breadth of vision that invention is possible. There's always a coherence in a genuine artistic point of view; designing a jacket or dreaming up the interior of a hotel are different sides of the same world. What counts is the vision, and I feel mine is clear-sighted. I'm focused and controlled, but behind the iciness is a hot-blooded and sensitive personality. I have learned to protect myself, otherwise the world might have taken advantage of me. I'm introverted and reserved: I have always preferred my studio to parties and social events, and even today I'm still the first to arrive at work in the morning and the last one to leave at night. I have found a way not to be overwhelmed by the indispensable performative side of my work: I have surrounded myself with a sort of mystique that some may interpret as being aloof, others as a role, others still as a form of shyness. And the last is the interpretation I like best.

COMMUNICATING

The greatest satisfaction for those of us in fashion is seeing the clothes we've designed worn by real people on the street. Of course, glossy publications and international red carpets are highly gratifying as well. Dressing a star for Oscar night is also a huge thrill, because stardust has something truly magical about it. I certainly don't want to lessen this aspect of my commitment as a fashion designer. However, touching the everyday side of people is a completely different kind of feeling, one that never stops motivating me to do better. Discovering that one of your jackets helped a woman feel confident about how she looked at a work meeting; seeing

GIORGIO ARMANI WOMEN, FALL/WINTER 1989–1990

a man wearing one of your suits walking as elegantly and as naturally as if he had nothing on: these are the real stimuli that I could never do without. Today, as in the past, fashion often seems to address only fashion insiders, suggesting absurd flights from reality. The fame I've achieved over the years has proven to me that I have always chosen the right channels and ways to speak to people. Communication, for anyone in fashion, is essential, especially today when we are overwhelmed by new products and styles. The creation of a memorable evening dress, a handbag that's a must-have, a blazer that's as comfortable as a cardigan, even a simple white T-shirt or a pair of jeans that captures the spirit of the moment: all these actions would be meaningless if they didn't reach the public in the right way. You need to communicate, to create an imagination, to mesmerize.

From the beginning of my career I have sought the most sophisticated and distinctive images, as if I have been a director of a long film for which each advertising campaign is a scene. My vision of style is all-encompassing: I can't imagine the clothes I design without a context. My aesthetic calls for specific scenarios, control over each and every detail: this is as true for the Giorgio Armani line as the experimental world of the Emporio; as much for the physical and muscular line of EA7 as it is for jeans. The metaphor of directing one long film for my career is no accident. In looking back at the sequences of the advertising campaigns, especially the first ones—so innovative and surprising—created together with Aldo Fallai, Peter Lindbergh, and other excellent photographers with the help of my sister Rosanna, who curated everything right alongside me, I realize that I have always pursued the utopia of the timeless image and realized it. It was natural for me to choose black-and-white film, which is always so pure and touching. That was when the foundations of my visual language were laid. Today, that language thrives on a dialogue with new photographers, and over the years it has taken on more incisive means of representation, ones more in tune with the times without ever losing its spirit, magic, or narrative charm. In communicating, for me, the focus is not so much on the clothes as it is on the attitudes that make them come alive, hence desirable: a self-aware and proud yet serene look. Style as a way of being.

I have always been unwilling to embrace exhibitionism, even in advertising. In the 1980s, when color was all the rage, I explored myriad shades of gray, casting yearning looks at 1940s movies, which have always struck me for their elegance and refinement. My images from that period continue to communicate profoundly, even though they were inexpensive to make. Even later when I chose color, I always rejected hues and combinations that were too much, too loud, too aggressive. Even the choice of models is essential to my fashion: I want character, not famous faces. Or rather, I want a famous face with character. I'm interested in the expressive

FOLLOWING PAGES: GIORGIO ARMANI WOMEN, FALL/WINTER 1987–1988; GIORGIO ARMANI CLASSICO, SPRING/SUMMER 1998

actor, not the fashion model riding the crest of the wave. My communication has also been based on bold choices, as well as my desire to break the mold. Like my mural in the heart of Milan. A single, gigantic image wedged into the urban fabric that speaks to everyone. It has been there since 1984. Some of my posters—the young bare-chested man holding a tiger cub in his hand or David Beckham wearing white underwear—have caused a scandal; others have confirmed, better than a thousand words, the spirit of the times. Others instead have been a message of encouragement, or a declaration of love for the city. Even today, I like that a solitary image can sum up the message of a season, just as I like the sense of expectation that the renewal of that immense mural creates in the passersby each time. When we first started, it was unusual for a fashion house to adopt such a sensational strategy, and maybe it still is today, but I have never been afraid to face the public at large. Elitism is foolish. This sense of reality is so important for me that today, at over eighty years of age, I'm proud of the signs that the passing of time have left on my body, and I'm willing to use my own face to endorse the projects that I cherish most of all.

REVOLUTIONIZING

It was never my conscious intention to revolutionize fashion, yet that is what happened. I'm not just referring to the fact that I freed men and women from rigidity, suggesting new attitudes instead. Soon, in fact, I decided to also turn to the world of young people, and to those who love fashion but can't afford it, thus experimenting with an unprecedented form of democracy. This decision shocked everyone at first, but it developed into yet another enduring success.

Many people criticized me when, in 1981, I opened my first Emporio Armani on Via Durini, just opposite my offices. It was filled with casual clothes, mostly made of denim, all at affordable prices and featuring an urban appeal. It was seen as being the wrong move in terms of marketing, an irreparable blow to my image. Was *the* fashion designer of the power woman and the new man really lowering himself to making things for the average Joe? How unfortunate. The prophets of doom, who are always quick to utter catastrophic judgments, believed that the new line would cannibalize the signature line. The symbol of the eagle was created because of a request made by Sergio, who called me to say he urgently needed to figure out a logo for the new line. So, while holding the phone in one hand and a pen in the other, I drew an eagle, which I felt symbolized the unattainable, and instead launched my name in the Olympus of the younger generation. I abhor designers who don't look at everyday reality. My jeans with the eagle logo soon became the symbol of belonging, and it was the same for my bomber jackets with the eagle emblazoned on the back. Wearing these clothes meant being part of a group, being faithful and true to them as well as yourself, so the jacket turned into something aspirational. The price was right, so Emporio mania soon took off. Emporio stores, both in Italy and abroad, multiplied, and the rest is history. One of the first signs of global fashion and of experimental aesthetics: the giant mural in the heart of Milan and *Emporio Armani Magazine*, a hybrid between a magazine and a catalogue, each represented a cutting-edge approach to the language of fashion, intertwining it with everything. Diversifying our production simultaneously rewarded us and made us credible, according to the many levels of the market. We designers come from industry, something we should never forget. Industry that has made the fashion system grow. From its first steps, Emporio Armani has become my favorite testing ground. By observing real life I understood which direction to take. The collection has a young feel, but it's not just for twenty-year-olds; instead, it's for those who, with taste and class, want to feel young at every age. This was also true for A/X, which I launched in 1991 in the United States with a store in New York that had an almost industrial feel to it and that focused on dressing the new urban generations. A line with a young, energetic spirit that has now become one of the three brands, the most dynamic and metro one, of the world of Armani, and that truly allows me to speak to the very young, in ways that are always open, always new, always straightforward. To the extent that for the opening of the store in Milan I recruited the staff via an open call on social media. Being connected with the street, with life, is everything for me, and the always enthusiastic reaction of the public is proof each time that I'm right.

CREATING FASHION

For me, fashion is an occupation that consists of equal parts imagination and pragmatism, insight and rigor, verve and control. There is nothing divine or sensational about it, yet it has an amazing impact on our everyday lives. In my pragmatic vision as an inventor, fashion isn't born from the song of the muses, a poetic sense of awe, or a creative frenzy. Creating fashion is a process of developing a coherent idea of beauty and sharing it with your public, keeping in mind the facts of contemporary life. If you're really careful, if you manage to intercept even the smallest of signals (the ones that are always there waiting for you), you'll understand the public's needs even before they materialize, and you'll spot the changes that are taking place in society before anyone else does.

GIORGIO ARMANI AT THE END OF THE
ONE NIGHT ONLY BEIJING SHOW, 2012

That's what happened to me at the beginning of my story. I was a young man who, like so many others, was experiencing the buzz of a decade of radical revolutions. Everything everywhere was changing, and it was changing fast. Women were becoming liberated. Men were abandoning their fathers' patterns of behavior and rules. All over, people were protesting the status quo. In hindsight, it was an age that was as exciting as it was difficult. This always happens during times of transition, when past certainties are replaced by new ideas and everything seems to waver. And yet I realized that liberation, both female and male, would only remain a marvelous theory, a half-baked revolution, if the proclamations and the progress weren't accompanied by new attitudes. I became convinced that those attitudes could be created out of the way people dressed. How was a woman rising up the ranks of power going to be credible, in an environment that was still all male, if she was dressed like a doll or restrained by excessively formal feminine clothing? How was a young, dynamic, and uninhibited man going to contrast with the old modes of thinking if he was constrained inside a suit that denied his individuality and oppressed his energy and physique? This discrepancy was what I decided to resolve. First and foremost, I decided to approach this with a kind of softness, aiming for a new harmony between the body and the garment, keeping in mind an essential point: clothing must bestow a sense of authority, elegance, and dignity without disguising each person's individuality. At the time I didn't feel like a champion or a provocateur; I was simply a creative with a vision, which I pursued. But I was sure I was right, and not for a single moment did I make a compromise. I was a forty-year-old man with salt-and-pepper hair who perceived the world around him acutely, and I responded, concretely, to the evident need for new types of clothes by proposing unstructured jackets, made out of loose and flowing fabrics. I used crepe, super-lightweight wool, and new, almost liquid-like fabric blends. I have the farsightedness of Nino Cerruti to thank: after hiring me to work for his company, he encouraged me to continue my investigations.

I was also fortunate to work with, and sometimes butt heads with, many fine Italian-American technicians who brought the American principles of manufacturing mass-produced clothing to Italy.

IMAGINING THE BODY

The body is both the point of departure and the point of arrival of everything I do. This might appear elementary, but it actually is quite profound. Very often in fashion, the body is only an abstraction on which designers imagine their fantasies; they try to show what has never been done before, some unattainable ideal to which to aspire fruitlessly, or else an entity that needs to be modified through outfits that look more like cages, traps, or superstructures. For me, and decades before me, for Paul Poiret and Coco Chanel, who took a stand against this very approach, this is an antiquated and often harmful way of understanding fashion. I love a naturalness that is synonymous with harmony, one that reveals the body's true energy. A body that is well taken care of but

GIORGIO ARMANI WOMEN, FALL/WINTER 1980–1981

accepted for what it is, with all its good qualities and all its faults, has more dignity than the excessively formal restraints imposed by some designers. As a young man I was deeply fascinated by the real body, both its mechanics and its subtle dynamics. That scientific respect for the body has never left me, and the same for my appreciation for the classic ideal of a man, the measure of all things: the expression of a physical balance that is, first and foremost, a mental well-being and clear thinking. Examples of this can be seen in the classical and neoclassical sculptures that I have tried to evoke in my advertising campaigns, with photographs that portray men with lithe and elegant muscles and slender and graceful women. These are extraordinary, global times, and so it's much easier now to accept the idea of different visions and ideals living in harmony; however, when I first started out, that was not the case, especially in the 1980s when diktats and aesthetic absolutism were the rule. The dominant look of the model back then was actually somewhat excessive and overbearing: men with body-builder muscles, women with bionic curves and the aggressive poses of predators. My point of view went in quite the opposite direction. The body was to be exalted in the name of an energetic naturalness, a vigorous sex appeal, a kind of pride that meant self-awareness, not exhibition. My self-possessed, dignified women had no need to flaunt a low neckline just to grab attention: after all, seduction is a game that brings a person closer, not a declaration of war. Back then everyone seemed to be shouting: "Look how beautiful we are." I always preferred the rustling of an essential elegance, the harmony of a perfect proportion. That was when I conceived the most traditional piece of clothing—the jacket—with a different formula.

I removed the stiffness that was inside to give it the suppleness of a cardigan and the lightness of a shirt, and I invented the unstructured jacket for both men and women. Now that manner of dressing has become classic, or rather "classic Armani." To achieve this, the public's approval has been crucial: I mean a real public, made up of ordinary men and women, as well as that of the up-and-coming star system. It was a whispered revolution, and for this reason truly efficient and enduring; it was a revolution built around the body, following its proportions and favoring its movements, where comfort is the goal. A revolutionary reimagining in which outfits of distinctive luxury offer each individual the true feeling of being him- or herself, but in the best way possible.

LOVING SPORTS

I love sports: the effort, the competition, the team spirit, the collaboration. Sports is about hard work. It's about effort. Lots of it. It's about, first and foremost, coming to terms with yourself and facing up to your limits, just for the sake of improving; pushing yourself as hard as you can and never giving up. The race is a test in which you participate—whether you win or not—and you always win when you put yourself on the line and use all the energy at your disposal intelligently. It's also about team spirit and working together to achieve a single goal, each teammate investing his or her talent, each setting aside ego in the name of a higher ideal.

In fashion, just as in sports, you need commitment and training. You don't compete just to win, but to express yourself. In the competition of fashion, what's important is originality, but above all what's important is having a vision and expressing it clearly so that the message will go straight to the point, like a swordsman, whose gestures must be decisive and fast to overcome the opponent, or a swimmer, whose strokes must be energetic and dynamic to be faster than the competitor. In the fashion race, just as in the sports race, it's important to see the opponent not as the enemy, but rather the stimulus to improve, to never give up, to not rest on your laurels. Being a part of my fashion team is like being on an Olympic team: what's important is to be coordinated, to collaborate. And, frankly, to accept the fact that I am the one who will make the decisions, just as a sports coach would. While some people might accuse me of being dictatorial, my achievements show that I've always been right.

EA7, the latest brand created by my organization, represents the ultimate expression of my sports mentality. The line I imagined for active sportswear combines the use of essential fabrics with a more modern look, but without the overly complicated innovations that are so typical of avant-garde designs. In comparison, I look for inspiration to the past, to sports clothing where you can clearly see, whispered in the details and the materials, the newest innovations at the time subtly integrated into the garments without ever departing from their elegant lines, as is often the case today through the exasperation of the theme: T-shirts with unnecessary frills, improbable shoes, overloaded with colors and details, designed for the most extreme consumerism.

ABOVE: GIORGIO ARMANI WITH GIOVANNI MALAGÒ
IN 2015 AT THE PRESENTATION OF THE UNIFORMS MADE
FOR THE OLYMPIC AND PARALYMPIC GAMES IN RIO 2016

LEFT: GIORGIO ARMANI WITH OLIMPIA MILANO TEAM
PLAYERS JERRY MCCULLOUGH, CLAUDIO COLDEBELLA,
AND JOSEPH BLAIR, 2004

REINVENTING GLAMOUR

What is glamour? Fascination, sensuousness, charm, beauty. It's a quality that attracts and intrigues, an allure that makes people special. It is seduction, which is usually associated in the collective imagination with a showy, conspicuous style that is far from the down-to-earth essence and subtle elegance I champion. And yet I love glamour. I first began exploring its potential and the richness of its nuances in the earliest stages of my career. I love a kind of precious and mysterious seduction, an ambience that reminds you of a scene in a movie. By following my instinct to combine a visual richness and rigor I have reinvented glamour, in my own special way. Over the years, I have shown that what's sexy is not a body laid bare before everyone's eyes: sexy is suggestion, a veiling and unveiling. It is allowing others to imagine, without explicitly showing.

Sometimes I feel that I fight a losing battle against some of the preconceptions about my work, but at this point in my career I can afford to ignore them as though they were just background noise (I actually always have). Some people try to compartmentalize my designs as a certain "look," owing to my precise style and preferences. For such people I am considered to merely be the designer of the kind of woman who wears a power suit in dull and dusty colors, so-called *greige*. You know, austere clothes, worn with flats—a certain sartorial androgyny. They completely ignore how varied my work is, and the diversity of my collections. They can't imagine a sparkling Armani who freely fantasizes, an exotic, dreamlike, eccentric Armani. But that Armani does exist, and he has his own public who acclaims him. I have invented a personal grammar of glamour, deconstructing stereotypes and clichés the way I had done at the beginning, when I got rid of the old-fashioned stiff uniform, adapting *his* jacket to *her* body and dissolving its pretension in a flowing and powerful line. This Armani is also free to contradict himself, to allow himself pleasures and digressions simply for the pleasure of doing so. Coherence is certainly one of my virtues—a personal and stylistic one—but being coherent does not mean getting stuck in a formula. We must seek change otherwise we risk getting stuck forever.

Over the course of the years, the glamour of certain movie stars has fueled my imagination: Greta Garbo and Marlene

Dietrich, unparalleled in their men's clothing and impeccable makeup. Cate Blanchett today, lunar and powerful. Lauren Bacall, Claudia Cardinale, Juliette Binoche. These are the examples that first come to mind when I think of my idea of glamour: women whose allure is a mixture of bearing and sensuousness; women whose total elegance is the polar opposite of disharmony. The glamour that I have evoked in recent years takes into account the great changes taking place in society. Women like Laura Morante, Margherita Buy, and Valeria Golino, as well as the more international looks of Alba Rohrwacher, Giovanna Mezzogiorno, Valeria Bruni, Kasia Smutniak, Natalie Portman, Naomi Watts, Cameron Diaz, Milla Jovovich, and Julia Roberts. These are women who, by rejecting regimented and conventional garb, offer us a less stereotyped image of iconic beauty.

In 2005, what a shock it was for everyone when I decided to venture into the domain, which was new for me, of haute couture, deciding, among other things, to show in Paris. Why would Armani, the Milanese fashion designer who has made pragmatism his credo, decide to try his hand at the frivolity of couture, an art believed to be on the road to extinction, in the city that has always been its cradle? Because I didn't want to limit the forms and ways in which I can express myself. Because there are women whose lives have dreams with specific needs, who love my style. I won't hide the fact that I considered freeing myself of the practical constraints of ready-to-wear fashion to be the last challenge left to me in terms of creativity. I wanted to show that delicate *greige* and seductive red can complement each other, that stiletto heels and men's shoes are elements of the same vision of style, that a sculptural hat and a tie are different accents of a single, very rich lexicon. And, after all, haute couture is not unfamiliar to an Italian designer: in representing the very peak of creativity, by not being restricted by pragmatic manufacturing concerns—only a limited number of outfits are made, created in ateliers not factories—haute couture affirms the excellence of craftsmanship that has always been a great Italian prerogative.

EXPERIENCING CINEMA

I have often wondered what my life would have been like without cinema. I certainly wouldn't be the man and the designer I am today. Cinema for me was not just a youthful passion that has continued into my adult life; it has also been a constant source of ideas and inspirations, a treasure trove of images that I draw upon to build my own world. Cinema is a repertoire of visions that have indelibly shaped my style and my way of understanding both the quality of elegance and communication. And it is through cinema that I first reached the public and entered into the collective imagination.

In today's media-saturated world, we are bombarded by all kinds of images, so it's hard to imagine the impact that the release of a movie could have had on the eyes and the imagination of a child or a young man like me: the sense of expectation it generated, the rapture that the images projected on gigantic screens created. It's even hard to imagine how mesmerizing the infinite shades of black and white were, how alluring their invitation to fantasize about invisible nuances and colors. (And what a surprise it was when Technicolor's bold colors arrived!) Today, between the TV and the Internet, we have nonstop access to film narratives, and while images can spread like wildfire, all too often true quality is missing. I belong to a generation for which cinema was the only form of entertainment: an all-encompassing yet eternally surprising one. In a postwar Italy that was much poorer than it is today, but also immensely more dignified, filled with opportunities for anyone who was gifted and determined enough to grab them and turn them into something real, cinema was a marvelous escape from reality, a chance to make fantasy come to life that was different from literature or theater, which also enthralled me. When I was a teenager, movies were basically American cowboy movies as well as musicals (which I couldn't stand), and the contrast between European and American cinematography was remarkable. Italian neorealism, with its beautifully made films, represented what we had actually experienced. So watching those movies was somehow disturbing because they reminded you of the adversities of the war that we had been through no more than a few years before. It was natural once I reached adulthood to recognize the value of that type of cinema, which certainly informed my choices as a fashion designer. At the movies, even the most fantastic scenes, the boldest flights of fantasy seem real: there they were, coming to life right before your eyes. At the movies, nothing was impossible, not even crossing space and time, battling a terrible monster, turning into an invisible man. Everything has changed since then, but it seems as though nothing has changed at all. My childhood dreams, my aspirations to become a director are now a reality. I finally found myself involved in the cinema, as an active protagonist and not just as a bewitched spectator. In 1980, a young director named Paul Schrader contacted me to clothe an actor who was not particularly famous at the time—Richard Gere—for a sensuous thriller called *American Gigolo*. I had no idea what the impact of that movie would be on the spirit of the 1980s, the powerful grip it would have on the public. The almost fetishistic sequence in which Richard as Julian Kay chooses what to wear from a closet filled with my creations was more penetrating and effective than a whole string of ads. It created, at an international level, the legend of Armani, because cinema leaves a deep mark in the imagination of moviegoers; it stirs their hidden desires. It was the start of a story that has lasted until today, and thanks to it I was able to meet filmmakers of the caliber of Martin Scorsese (who also made a film about me called *Made in Milan*), Brian De Palma, Bernardo Bertolucci, Giuseppe Tornatore, and Paolo Sorrentino, to name just a few. Since then, I have contributed to movies of all kinds: the fantastic in *The Dark Knight*, directed by Christopher Nolan; the historical in *The Untouchables*, by Brian De Palma; and the brutal in *Streets of Fire*, directed by Walter Hill. My conversation with cinema has been a common thread, step by step, throughout my career. When a filmmaker calls me, I always evaluate the project carefully. In fact, cinema allows me to work with clothes in a way that upholds my vision of style, in that I help to build a character. It's the kind of operation that, when it really works out well, rewards you in the most satisfying of ways: eternity. A successful character surpasses the barrier of time; he or she becomes a legendary figure and not just because of the way they act, but because of the way they're dressed.

What would Dick Tracy be without his fedora, Julian Kay without his unstructured jacket, or Jimmy Malone without his tweed vest and wool cloth cap?

MEETING THE STARS

My experience in cinema happened spontaneously, without strategies drawn up beforehand or plans astutely calculated by publicists or marketing and PR people. In the stars of the moment I saw the image of a new cinema, and in me—or, rather, the clothes I designed—they saw their own desire to look utterly distinctive. It was a pioneering approach. Before then the fashion created by designers and that of international red carpets never mingled; Hollywood resorted to costume designers and the solemn, unattainable theatrical image of "The Star." But the young actors that were about to come into the limelight in the late 1970s had other ambitions and expectations, and a wholly different idea of their own image. They were uninhibited, real, even proud of their short-comings; they didn't think of stardom as some mystical experience but instead with a kind of conscious disenchantment. I'm thinking of Diane Keaton. Lauren Hutton. Richard Gere, Robert De Niro, Al Pacino, and later, Russell Crowe, George Clooney, Michelle Pfeiffer, Jodie Foster, Glenn Close, Helen Mirren, and many others. Men and women, beyond being actors and actresses, searching, like everyone at the time, for a new way of presenting themselves on the social and professional scenes. Starting with *American Gigolo*, these men and women turned to me with a kind of intuitive understanding of how the natural, essential elegance of my styles would help them maintain their status as stars without everything turning into some sort of circus, which is the way it used to happen—and I say this without passing any judgment on Old Hollywood, whose potent imaginary world I have always admired and whose power of seduction enmeshed and surprised me as a young man. But times change. Every era resorts to new aesthetic "tools." Today, the red carpets have become a marketing strategy, and many fashion houses choose stars simply because they are in the limelight at that moment. I have instead always preferred to do things my own way, which is, first and foremost, to create a human relationship and a deeply personal understanding.

FOLLOWING PAGES: GIORGIO ARMANI WITH CLAUDIA CARDINALE
IN PANTELLERIA, 1990S; GIORGIO ARMANI WITH SOPHIA LOREN, 2005

SHOWING

Even after more than forty years, nothing has changed for me. The fashion show will always be a magical moment, fear of not being able to succeed, the ultimate trial by fire. Each show gives me a thrill: it's the same feeling I had when I started out, in spite of the fact that I have by this time done hundreds of them. I don't fall to pieces, one reason being I can't stand people who get hysterical, but I must admit the apprehension is there. It's not that I'm insecure about what I've created—I've always firmly believed in my ideas and I'm unafraid to take them forward at any cost. But I've always felt that showing your work is a lot like being naked (however paradoxical that may seem, seeing as we're talking about clothing, not nudity). Each show is like taking final exams before a public made up of journalists and buyers, as well as friends, stars, and collaborators whom I don't want to let down. I always think "oh, I'm not nervous," until the very second the first model steps out onto the catwalk. From that moment, the doubt of not having succeeded arises. There's the unknown, the criticism and the attacks that, even though they're restrained (undoubtedly out of a form of respect), my sensibility can still detect. It's true that we work behind closed

RUNWAY SEASON FINALE, GIORGIO ARMANI PRIVÉ,
AT ARMANI HOTEL DUBAI, SPRING/SUMMER 2010

doors for six months to face, through a fashion show, the eyes and judgment of the public. It is that magical and spectacular split second when the ensembles, on models and mannequins, come alive and acquire a presence. The fashion show is the message you launch at the world: it's the first, and the strongest. I like to think of fashion as a job in which you explore the fourth dimension: clothing and accessories are objects with shape and substance, but it's only with movement—the fourth dimension—that they reveal their true worth. The movement of the mannequin and the model completes the designer's work, and it's the kind of movement that can never be fully perceived and truly captured on a video that records the images. This is why, even though everyone today is calling for an end to fashion shows, I believe they are still a crucial tool. All of us realized this during the two years of the pandemic. Even the best video possible, the most enthralling one, is nothing compared to a fashion show. Of course, a video allows us to reach a larger audience, because never before is the fashion public global. A show is an exercise that requires a great deal of concentration and directing skills in the use of specific means, from the casting to the makeup and hairstyling of the models to, lastly, the use of lighting, visual effects, and music. A striking example about the importance of music for a show comes to mind: as one of our first debut shows was about to end, the lights not yet dimming on the catwalk, the models were dressed in a very thin gauze that was quite colorful but actually poor in quality. At the time we didn't have much money to invest in the clothing, so for that collection we had decided to use felt-tip markers to hand-print a whole piece of white linen, which we would then use to make the clothes for the show. The show was close to the finale but we thought something was missing. So Sergio, who was with me, randomly chose a record, without giving it too much thought. It was music by the Chilean folk group Inti-Illimani. And with that music, the finale became miraculous, and that show was remembered for a long time afterward. Backstage at my fashion shows, I prowl around like a restless cat in a basket it's not familiar with. Each time it's different, but the rituals are the same: I always wear blue trousers and a blue T-shirt and sneakers, even though every time I resolve to wear a different outfit to thank the public. The alternatives would be a formal jacket, a polo shirt, or, something I've worn before, the kind of white T-shirt a pizzamaker wears, but that has always been my uniform for both work and life. I always make sure that the people responsible for the style office are in attendance, like Leo, Silvana, and their collaborators. If Paul, my first secretary and assistant, isn't there, then I call him, even when I don't have anything particular I need to ask him about. It's enough to have him nearby. Then there's Irene, my legendary secretary from the days when I started out on Corso Venezia, who has always lined up the models and called them by name in the order in which they go out. Despite the fact that there are people employed to do so officially, for the whole time she's present backstage

FOLLOWING PAGES: RUNWAY SEASON FINALE,
GIORGIO ARMANI PRIVÉ, SPRING/SUMMER 2009

it's like a talismanic rite. Not hearing her loud voice shouting out "Penelope, Chantal, Olga!" before the show would certainly mean trouble is brewing. Roberta, my niece, who deals with the celebrities, is busy seeing to the usual group, with the same concerns. There are photographers and videographers, even for this small performance. I'm restless, but I try to create a rapport with the models who, little by little, as they shed their toughness as professionals, fall prey to the charm of yours truly. An hour before the event, I have already explained to them how to move on those yards of lit-up catwalk, how to hold their handbags, how to look out into the audience without letting it show too much. As if by magic, from the confusion backstage, with the photographers taking pictures for their reporting, the makeup artists adding the final touches, the models who ignore them as they check themselves out in front of the mirror, adjusting a collar rather than their belt, when I give the signal everything starts and complete silence falls. I'm responsible for the direction, the lights, and the music. The catwalk isn't lit up yet and there are still some empty seats in the first VIP row. So slightly more peremptorily, using Paul as a go-between, I send Roberta a message: "Roby, don't take too long with the celebrities!" Without being seen, from the small dark corridor that separates us from the catwalk, I spray some of my personal perfume on the girls. One of the girls, before going out, has a moment's hesitation. I gently touch her at the waist with both hands to reassure her, the music starts, and off we go.

DRAWING

I'm never satisfied. I could also have done something different in life other than fashion. Who knows: after all, our lives are the product of a succession of unpredictable events. Whatever professional field I had chosen, however, I am sure I would have done my best to succeed and realize my ideas and aspirations. In fact, as someone who is forever dissatisfied and obsessive in his search for perfection, I never give up until I've achieved the results I want. I like this continuous challenge, so much so that sometimes the process of developing an idea excites me even more than arriving at the final product. I like the feeling of an idea being born. I like to hone it, change it, correct it, and then, in the end, transform it into something concrete. I've never taken drugs, yet for me the surge of adrenaline I get from my work is better than any hallucination or artificial high. It's a kind of orgasm (if I may use this expression). Drawing is one such source of pleasure–it's also one of the most important phases in my work and unquestionably the most intense and gratifying. It's a passion, a moment of dialogue with myself, and a kind of research.

As a designer, it's not enough to know how to sew; you have to be able to follow a specific line of thought, and drawing is, at its basis, thinking. People underestimate the importance of drawing in fashion. But to those who insist that all you need is a computer, I reply that then the essential human factor is missing: the hand that traces the width of a pair of pants or how low the neckline on an evening dress should be.

An accurately drawn pencil line clarifies to the dressmaker just how that dress should fall on the mannequin's body. I've always drawn as part of my work. The figures I drew before I started my career were very spontaneous; I used white paper for the summer and black paper for the winter, with a few quick, lively lines made in color. When I look at my drawings today, I find them almost touching: I see myself bent upon affirming my vision, which was so different from what was around me. While the drawings I make now are more realistic and professional (and they couldn't be otherwise, in light of the experience I've built up), over the years one feature has stayed the same: their capacity for synthesis, the ability to capture on paper an item of clothing that is identical to the one that I will eventually create. My path to a new creation starts with just a few lines sketched on paper and ends with an image comprising a select number of elements combined in a subtle way. Simple yes, but the kind of simplicity that evokes strength. Simplicity is never the point of departure; it's the point of arrival.

GIORGIO ARMANI WOMEN'S COLLECTION,
FALL/WINTER 1992–1993

GIORGIO ARMANI MEN'S COLLECTION,
FALL/WINTER 2002-2003

FANTASIZING

In my quest to discover pure fashion—ensembles that have both the timeless perfection of the archetype and the kind of absolute elegance that transcends history—I have always felt an intuitive affinity with distant cultures. There is a special sort of allure in the traditional costumes worn by different peoples, in their distinctive decoration and line, in their richness of color, and in their unique wearability. There's also poetry in them, at least to my eyes, as someone who travels in his imagination, someone who fantasizes, letting himself be transported on the waves of thinking and style.

I love the Far East: Japan, of course, as well as China. I love the surprising hues, the prints and engravings, the charming asymmetries and severe gracefulness. But I also love the

GIORGIO ARMANI TRAVELING THROUGH INDIA, 1995

Southern and Eastern parts of the world, the Polynesia of Gauguin and the traditions of the Mediterranean basin, such as those of sun-scorched Africa, characterized by an austere and ancestral opulence. I avoid merely copying traditional forms, styles, and decorations, preferring instead to explore a reinterpretation that is both decisive and nuanced. *Echi di etnie*, "Ethnic Echoes," is what I named a recent haute couture collection, one brimming with the recognizable signs of other cultures. Maghrebian forms, Middle Eastern traces, African prints, and Western cuts blended in a strongly evocative visual weaving. This is my personal idea of exoticism: imagining and reinterpreting an "elsewhere," capturing its purity, its capacity to move the soul.

These signs and subtle traces have always crossed my work, at the heart of its softest and most feminine side, but also its richest and most fanciful. Exoticism is my idea of escaping from reality into dreams, all the while keeping my feet firmly rooted to the ground. While I love the graceful yet rigorous exploration of the infinite variations in menswear interpreted in a feminine style—one that dresses the working woman and offers new tools for self-representation—I also love just letting myself go and dreaming. But these two approaches are not mutually exclusive; rather, they compensate for and complete each other. I have never loved creativity for its own sake, that explosion of imagination that results in creations that have nothing wearable about them.

For me, even the highest flight of fancy has to make sense. It has to be translatable into clothing or an accessory that a woman or a man will be able to wear.

This longing to fantasize, to look beyond the horizon (not unlike what Paul Poiret, whom I consider to be the absolute master of exoticism, did in his day and age) has kept me company ever since I first began my career as a designer. This longing has informed important stages in my work, starting from the 1981 Japanese collection. This collection, deeply inspired by the prints of Utamaro, was characterized by armor-like forms and by a whole new taste—unprecedented for me—for bright colors. I have since returned to Japan on a number of occasions, and have created an entire collection called Privè in tribute to this country whose aesthetics are so refined and unique. In other collections, at other times, dabs of China, Persia, Syria, and Arabia appear and reappear.

Sometimes it's just a trace of color: an unexpected and saturated nuance on a sea of gray, or a Tuareg blue that pervades and transfigures the clothes. I do not force any limits upon my imagination. I like to fantasize; looking beyond is an intense and gratifying way to reinvent what I create here and now.

BEING EXHIBITED

Strange fate, mine: I have always said that fashion is not art, and yet I was the first and I think the only fashion designer to be exhibited at the Solomon R. Guggenheim Museum in New York. In 2000, that contemporary art institution dedicated a retrospective to my work, analyzing it as one would that of a painter, architect, or inventor. The museum's acknowledgment of my practice touched me deeply, because it singled out and unveiled my contribution to culture and society in a moment of renewal. I stubbornly remain convinced that fashion is not an art form. Art, real art with a capital A, is made to last. It transcends time and sums up a society's highest aesthetic and cultural values. In contrast, fashion is created, consumed, and renewed in a quick and endless cycle. Fashion is linked to the everyday. It has to do with habits, with customs and consumption, with people's roles, with the representation of the individual as well as of the community. It's a very important expression of the culture of every population, an aspect that has grown even more important in the global world we live in today. But all the same, at most it is an applied art. Fashion creations must be beautiful, of course, but they must first of all fulfill a function, whereas in art there is no function, only aesthetics. What good would a jacket with six sleeves be, or a pair of trousers with three legs, or a fantastic and spectacular dress in which you can't move, or a pair of shoes with a sensational design but are unsuitable for walking? There you are. I've always seen my role as fashion designer as being closer to that of a sociologist than that of an artist. I've always offered my public, which is varied because every type of product is included in the world, new tools of emancipation and self-representation, tools capable of giving new meaning to daily gestures. Perhaps in this sense I have been discreetly revolutionary. But one thing is for sure: I don't see myself as an artist. To go back to the Guggenheim retrospective, the exhibition that Harold Koda and Germano Celant curated with acumen, selecting more than five hundred pieces from my archive, touched upon what is at the heart of my work on the line and the material without shrouding me in the aura of the Great Artist. Instead, it cast me as a lucid, inspired, pragmatic, and even visionary designer. I also had the privilege of collaborating with the installation of the show with my friend Robert Wilson, who choreographed the visual environment in inventive, surprising ways, making the viewers feel as though they were inside a paper Noguchi lamp. Michael Galasso created an all-encompassing collage of sounds, as if sculpting the air and the atmosphere around the clothes. An exhibition can be seen in two different ways. On the one hand, there's the immediate satisfaction of the creator's ego. On the other, there's the educational value, the unique testimony that is offered not only to the public through your work, but above all to young creatives: it is a feeling that lasts and is gratifying. I'm interested in this second aspect. I would like my very long career and my very rich experiences to serve as a guide, to prompt those who are determined and capable of doing the same. For this reason I conceived a vast space in Milan for a museum and archive, measuring more than 32,000 square feet, in which to collect all my drawings, clothes, products, and concepts. I named it Armani Silos, in tribute to the original use of this building, which stored food. Just as a silo is a container for life's essential needs, clothes are essential to life. I displayed my work here, but I also used the space to create a new dialogue with the city of Milan, organizing photography and architecture exhibitions, film festivals, and much more. I am happy to have been able to contribute with

Silos, in my own way, to including fashion in the country's cultural fabric. However much it is an important, actually crucial voice in our economy, fashion still has an inferiority complex. It is looked down upon, as though it were a purely commercial activity, when instead fashion has so much to say about the culture of a specific era, about dominant values, and about the idea of modernity. In Milan, and throughout Italy, there is still no fashion museum, while there is one in Paris. Nevertheless, Silos is not an attempt to replace the institutions, rather, it is meant to be the start of a conversation.

FOLLOWING PAGES: ARMANI/SILOS, APRIL 2015

DEFINING A LIFESTYLE

I started out by creating clothes, and, one step at a time, I have ventured beyond that. My name appears on a line of cosmetics and fragrances that have become a substantial articulation of my vision. I create furnishings. I have designed the interior decor of two hotels, which I have also given my name to, one in Milan and another in Dubai: these stand as the utmost expression of my way of understanding space and the elegance of an environment. They also are the expression of the kind of discreet and sophisticated sociability found in prestigious residences in many parts of the world and private homes. I have opened coffee houses around the world, places where people can relax and meet other people.

From jeans to underwear, from haute couture to handbags and watches, I offer a piece of my vision to everyone, making no distinctions and always with the same creative rigor. I have put my brand on desserts, and I create sports gear for athletes while sponsoring the teams. I collaborate with young filmmakers. I invent other ways, both digital and material, to interact with my public. I support charity events and organize competitions. In Milan, I have taken an active part in making sure that the new generation of fashion designers has the visibility it needs, offering my theater each season to someone who is just starting out in this field. I create events all around the world. While I move in different, seemingly antithetical spheres, I am stimulated by what I do, and the only rule I follow is that of instinct. Whenever I perceive a new challenge that could lead to my creative enrichment, as well as being of entrepreneurial interest, I take the figurative bull by the horns. Decisions get made naturally, with the unfettered mind of the creator and the pragmatism of the businessman. That the results are as coherent as they are lies in my method: I deal with projects in my own individual way, and this "Armanizes" everything, producing results that are cohesive yet varied as well.

At this point in my career, and in today's global scenario, being called a fashion designer is perhaps too narrow a term. Yet it's the only name with which I can truly identify. A *stilista*, literally, is a creator of styles, whether he or she is dealing with a garment or a car—basically, a creator of an entire style of life. And I have indeed invented a new lifestyle, a new way of being. After all, fashion means manner: a manner of offering oneself, of moving, of living. What counts in life is integrity, and everything I have done outside of fashion has integrity because behind it is my eye and behind that is my taste. If I were to describe my concept of lifestyle, I'd say that it thrives on humanistic harmony: every single expression of style places the person at the very heart—not the outfit or the accessory, the room he or she inhabits, or the signs of social status and well-being that surround this person. Everything is meticulously integrated so that it all comes together naturally, thus bringing an intelligence and sensibility to what is at the center: the body. The Armani lifestyle is the exact opposite of ostentation; it is made up of stylized elements, precious materials, subtle colors, even when my eclecticism has made me put forward, on various occasions, solutions that have a more forceful, unusual impact. For many it is a luxurious lifestyle; however, "luxury" is a word I don't care for much these days. It has become a flat concept, no more than a layer of veneer to make products and ideas that don't at all deserve to be defined as such more appealing. Luxury cannot be reduced to a formula. My lifestyle is positive and healthy; it uses only the finest materials, imbuing them with elegance and sophistication. It is a flawless distillation of the values that make us human and elevate us.

LIVING

Rigor, constancy, and method are just one side of my persona. There is great complexity behind appearances. I always say that if I were less judicious, if I had been less interested in proving myself and if my work hadn't been so dominant, I would probably have led the life of a nomad. I would have followed those hippies who, in the early years of my career, I watched from a distance as they rejected the bourgeois lifestyle and gave everything up to pursue alternate paths. It's a thought that lasts about a second, of course: I really can't picture myself traveling the world, my hair long and a knapsack on my back. But there is one thing about my inner nomadism that has remained: in every place I visited I would have liked to have a house. It's the only indulgence I actually allow myself, the only pleasure as a famous man. On second thought, I am the exact opposite of the hippie with wanderlust. I need to live in a familiar space, on which I have left my personal mark.

A house for me is not a solitary den, isolated from everything else; I like to see it alive and filled with friends with whom I share my time, experiences, and conversation. People say I'm introverted, and it's true that I don't socialize much. But I do like to entertain, I really do! And this is true for my home in Milan, just as it is for the one I own in Pantelleria, where I spend memorable summers. It's also true for my homes in Broni, Paris, Antigua, Saint-Moritz, New York, Saint-Tropez, and Forte dei Marmi. Each house is different because each location is, too, and I like to respect the essential characteristics of each region. But the style and interior decor are the products of the same formula that I apply to my fashion, as are my effortless rigor, my desire for simplicity and warmth.

I'm the one who conceives them and I'm also the one who decorates them (with a strong aesthetic sense like mine, handing my trust over to the whims of an architect would be rather traumatic or an all-out battle, with all my respect for the professionals who have played a part in my choices).

I like big spaces where you can find a more private corner to live in day after day. I detest having things hanging on the walls, and in fact the walls in my houses are often bare. I have forced myself not to collect art, except for two very small pieces that I received as gifts—a drawing by Henri Matisse and a photograph by Man Ray—because I think that masterpieces should be kept in museums and not be the property of an individual for his or her egotistical pleasure. I like furniture with essential lines, where what speaks is the naked beauty of the materials and the quintessence of the lines. I keep well in mind the teachings of Jean-Michel Frank, an architect whom I admire and identify with. When I launched my Armani/Casa collection, there were many who were surprised, but for me it was simply the logical extension of what I was already doing at a personal level: I offered my public the chance not to just wear my clothes, but to live the way I suggest they do, as well.

Via Borgonuovo is my most recognizable home: it's where I've been living for a long time and where I work. It's a small, winding street in Milan's Brera neighborhood, where the reserved discretion of the facades and the hidden splendor of courtyard gardens capture the spirit of what it means to be truly Milanese. The other place in my heart is my property in Pantelleria, where I can experience the joy of the sea and the sun—my elements—joined in a landscape scorched by the light and the wind. I'm enthralled by the idea of living on the frontier between different civilizations, between Europe and Africa.

FOLLOWING PAGES: THE HOUSE IN MILAN WITH
THE GORILLA WORK BY MARCANTONIO, 2012;
THE HOUSE IN PANTELLERIA, 2002

BEING FAMOUS

I have always accepted fame as an obligation, as the consequence of an important commitment, something I have always wanted even if it meant undertaking an arduous journey. It is the result of hard, intense, impassioned work that has never afforded me any respite. I have always been too pragmatic to think of fame as though it were some trinket, or flaunting it like a sparkling jewel.

No doubt my world acclaim is always right there, looming over me, preceding me wherever I go, and sometimes overwhelming me wherever I end up. However, it is true that I achieved it because of my merits in the field, and the endorsements I have been given fill me with pride. Exclusive publications, the editorials of prestigious newspapers, and in-depth illustrated magazines. The most striking example is the cover story that *Time* magazine dedicated to me and that, in spite of the fact that I was fully aware of what it meant to accept an interview with their reporter, still caught me by surprise on the occasion of my fashion show in Paris. The amusing part is that it was the great Italian couturier Valentino who made me realize just how important the cover was when, while running into each other at the exit from Plaza Athénée, he shouted out "però!"—an Italian exclamation of congratulations. I have learned to experience fame with a kind of detachment, aware of the fact that each test the star system subjects you to means you will be judged. Being famous is almost a moral commitment, to not compromise yourself, to hold the confidence of those who believe in you, to always maintain your signature style, with the conviction that in life being famous means being famous forever. And it also means setting an example for others, but also giving back. I realized this during the difficult period of the pandemic: a time that put the individual and the community, each of us and all of us together, to the test. During those difficult months I was very busy and concretely involved in making donations and productive reconversions, not for the purpose of exploiting what is good as a vehicle of communication, but in order to offer support and relief. I believe that ethical behavior is the absolute duty of all those who are famous.

CHINA'S 100 RICHEST BUSINESSPEOPLE

November 12, 2001
www.forbes.com

Forbes
global

Designer
Giorgio Armani
has built a
billion-dollar
fashion business.
Can it outlast him?

One
Man
Brand
PAGE 42

Argentina	Peso 8.00	Germany	DM 11.00	México	Peso 35	Spain	Ptas 875

ABOVE: GIORGIO ARMANI ON THE COVER OF *FORBES*, 2001;
RIGHT: GIORGIO ARMANI ON THE COVER OF *TIME*, 1982

148

$1.50

TIME

Giorgio's Gorgeous Style

Fashion Designer
Giorgio Armani

BEING THERE

I travel a lot, but more for work than for pleasure. I travel to places both far-flung and quite close. East, west, north, south. To new markets and markets that have by now become established. Official events, award ceremonies, retrospective fashion shows, exhibitions, tributes, celebrations, openings. I'm always there, in spite of my countless commitments as a designer and an entrepreneur, because I'm convinced that it's important to establish a real dialogue between the creator and the public, and that nothing strengthens this dialogue more than one's presence, however distant or exotic that place may be.

People love to see you in the flesh, ready to answer questions, ready to be photographed and to explain what lies behind your choices, whether style or lifestyle. We are living in a world that is becoming increasingly virtual. Personal relationships are filtered by the coldness of a screen, behind which one can easily hide, waiving the chance to risk and thus to gain. It's hard to resist this very impersonal culture, even though it's not an integral part of me. I still think there's a great need for authentic relationships, for a physical and tangible humanity, for gazes right in the eye and firm handshakes, instead of likes and posts on social media. Being there means making a huge effort, it's true, but that is something I don't want to give up for any reason whatsoever, because being there is a way of showing the public just how much humanity, strength, and passion underlie everything I do. And besides that, traveling is a great opportunity: it opens the mind and broadens the horizons.

I have been fortunate to do what I love and what has made me famous around the world. I always manage to transform even the busiest trips, even the quickest visits, into an opportunity for personal enrichment—even more so than for professional enrichment—for inspiration and growth. Hanging on the walls of my offices in Milan, in the meeting rooms, are maps of every continent. On each one, tiny flags mark the presence of my stores, or in any case, outposts. There are a lot of them, and often in the most unexpected places. I want the public, wherever they are—in Beijing or London, Tokyo or New York, Rome or Moscow—to be transported to the center of my world, to appreciate its sound and fragrances, to capture its essence. I want this to happen through events that bestow a physical presence on my work, that make it visible on living bodies in movement. It should come as no surprise that I named my famous series of traveling events *One Night Only*: just one night to involve the public in something special, to accompany them on a fantastic voyage, to surprise them, amuse them, and inspire them. Every *One Night Only* lets me enter into conversation with each place, to choose the means of expression, the locations, to work out ever new and ever different solutions, from the imposing architecture of the Esposizione Universale di Roma to the piers of industrial New York, a symbol of creative and cultural ferment, to a former gasholder in Beijing's hottest art district or to my hotel in Dubai. By reinventing the fashion show in places like these, my message becomes fluid, all embracing, and transformative. I was one of the first to understand the global importance of fashion, and these events definitively portray how the same vision can be relevant for far-ranging cities and cultures, no matter how distant or seemingly antithetical. It's a local strategy to achieve global action. The acknowledgments I have received have been and are for various reasons.

I realized the importance of this visionary approach in what was one of my very first business trips: it was a memorable experience. The year was 1979 and I had won the Neiman Marcus Award in New York. At the same time, Saks Fifth Avenue had organized a trunk show of my collection. The sheer size of the crowds turned what was supposed to be a small fashion show for just a limited group of loyal customers into an event that was repeated over several days. It was the start of my success, of my love story with the United States, and the first sign that traveling was going to give me a solid reputation, the kind that is etched both in time and actions. Since then, I have never stopped moving around, with the same passion and curiosity as ever. And that journey has brought me to where I am now, through myriad unique experiences. I even had a show in a hangar at Linate Airport, with Emporio Armani, reinforcing my connection to Milan and underscoring the overwhelming force of European power.

FOLLOWING PAGES: MODELS BACKSTAGE AT THE GIORGIO ARMANI PRIVÉ SHOW, SPRING/SUMMER 2014, *ONE NIGHT ONLY NEW YORK CITY*, OCTOBER 2013

GIORGIO ARMANI

ONE
NIGHT
ONLY

NEW YORK CITY

DISCOVERING ONE'S OWN ECCENTRICITY

Precise, meticulous, rigorous, uncompromising, loyal, constant, determined, passionate: these are the adjectives I identify with, as a person and as a fashion designer. My fashion starts from a kind of intense deduction, first discerning who might be the person wearing the garment and next, distilling from that a lasting style that is also capable of evolving. All this rigor and intense focus have earned for my work a minimalist label, although I don't identify myself like that, at least not completely. I don't identify myself by labels at all, not even in schools of thought, as labels dismiss the sheer variety of inspirations; they level out the pathways of the mind and impose blind obedience to pre-established principles.

I have always felt like an outsider in regard to the fashion system, not being particularly interested in the idea that radical renewal every six months is of value, and I am not at all inclined to follow the dominant trends and representations of seduction and femininity. I am allergic to the fireworks of fake revolutions that fizzle out in the time it takes to see the fashion show. I prefer to experiment by following my own pace, create my own style by obeying the rules that pertain to me alone, define an aesthetic that is all and only mine. I want to be myself. In other words, I am eccentric, and I say this with pride, even though the adjective sometimes associated with crazy, might seem light-years away from what I do. It has taken me a long time to discover that that's the way I am. The word "eccentric" isn't necessarily a synonym for flamboyant, theatrical, or excessive. Eccentric, if anything, means radical: this is how I have been called on more than one occasion, because of my ideas. Being eccentric literally means moving away from the center, and it connotes something outside of the box, unconventional, unorthodox. Eccentric to me means the rigor of absolute purism, waiving any form of decoration, or at least the studied overabundance of decorations. Eccentricity is independence both in thought and in action. I have more than forty years of collections that are proof of this independence. I have a whole body of special clothes and fantastic inventions to offer as examples. I have put them on view and exhibited them around the world for the pleasure of showing the other Armani, the one capable of toying with the image, of weaving subtle patterns of cross-references and allusions. That is the eccentric Armani: rigorous in my method and free in my results.

Being eccentric, for me, is an unconventional way of looking at a garment and its context, of playing with proportions and details. It doesn't take much for the effect to be surprising. A jeweled insect or graphic black and white that creates silhouettes that trick the eye; a unique hat, or a magical combination of colors; an embroidered men's pinstripe, or snakeskin scales turned into an intriguing surface. An unorthodox attitude is what makes something eccentric, not following a formula. My work, especially in the beginning, was already powerfully eccentric: I created a women's version of a man's suit, offsetting that suit's so-called masculine sobriety with the lighthearted, casual irreverence of what protestors of the time were wearing or the exact opposite of what was then the dominant way of thinking. The fact that eccentricity turned me into an institution is proof, incidentally, that thinking outside of the box is essential for success.

With the exhibition *Eccentrico*, which combines the most significant part of my work in the ready-to-wear sector with couture, I have wanted to show that there can be a link between serious intent and eccentricity, and that for me, it has been this way from the beginning. My eccentricity is, so to speak, Armanian: decisive yet subtle. Inspired by the freedom of thought and the artistic integrity of such true eccentrics as Jean Cocteau, Jean-Michel Frank, Elsa Schiaparelli, and Coco Chanel, my taste for eccentricity has paralleled my sense of rigor. At first, I focused my attention on line, favoring the profound societal change that was underway, offering women the unusual elegance of pantsuits. Then I explored other territories as I saw these liberated women coming to terms with their freer, lighter side. Perhaps a person is born eccentric. Or else, perhaps, you discover that you're like that, which is what happened to me. It's a path that has also represented the achievement of a new sense of freedom. It's the same freedom that, as a designer committed to creating hundreds of pieces of clothing year in and year out, I myself experience by donning my own personal uniform, which is always the same: blue . . . which, if you think about it, is truly an absolutely rigorous form of eccentricity.

FOLLOWING PAGES: GIORGIO ARMANI PRIVÉ,
ECCENTRICO EXHIBITION, PARIS, JANUARY 2014

ETHICS AS AESTHETICS

A great renewal is underway in society at this very moment. The climate is different and the environmental priorities are clear to see, but I feel as though I am living once again in the exciting atmosphere of the 1970s when I was just getting started. At the time, fashion was side-by-side with the liberation movement. Today, fashion can contribute to improvements by realigning itself to people's real needs, respecting the common goods that need to be protected: the social fabric and the environment. These are important values in which I have always believed, and that I have always defended. I have created a style through which, with great coherence,

I have continued for years to explore the countless changes and possibilities. To the extent that it is an expression of a precise vision down to the smallest detail, mine is a style in the original sense of the word: it is a way of being and of presenting oneself, certainly made up of clothes and accessories, but also of manners, gestures, interests, and attitudes. A style that goes beyond the sum of the parts that it consists of, and that goes well beyond what we wear. I am convinced that ethics and aesthetics must coincide, and this is why I express long-lasting and fundamental values through style. I do so by creating timeless objects that pure and essential design, accentuated by precious materials and artisanship, subtracts from the fleetingness of short-lived fashions. Clothes that emphasize fluidity that is as much the softness of the way they are made as the natural and progressive fusion of male and female codes, thus expressing a mysterious, personal femininity and a tender, knowing masculinity. I created my style starting from the body, dressing it tenderly, turning comfort into an undisputable feature. I imagine clothes that are discreet, that are never needlessly showy; clothes that are pleasant to wear, that follow the wearer's movements naturally. Clothes that fulfill a function, elegantly so. In every aspect of my work I put the person at the center, to whom I offer clothes that are an instrument for a new representation of the self: the power suit worn by women who have by now become the protagonists of the world of work; the soft suit worn by men who are far-removed from the rigid idea of the masculine, an idea that has been surpassed. I believe in an idea of inclusion that is, firstly, that of the mind: by rejecting the idea of the mainstream status symbol, I speak to independent personalities, intelligent characters, and I offer creations that last in time because they are born from the idea that less is better, that is, from the firm belief that good design has no expiration date and has nothing to do with irresponsible consumerism. Style as a way of living sustainably: that is how I define my contribution to today's world. I consolidate this vision through the extreme discipline of the designer who is first of all intransigent with himself, caught up in a challenge aimed at ongoing improvement that today cannot ignore the respect for the environment, and then, above all, by way of independence, a basic feature that is strenuously defended, the sole fuel for a free and personal expression, for authenticity that has turned my style into a lifestyle, an idea of ethics as aesthetics.

TELLING IT LIKE IT IS

On April 3, 2020, a new phase started for me, one I am still pursuing. I was in Forte dei Marmi, in lockdown with my family and closest collaborators, uncertain about the future, concerned about the events that had caught us off-guard, determined to find a solution that would not be just theory or nice words. While reading an article in *WWD*, an important periodical in my sector, I had a powerful gut reaction. I took out a sheet of paper and a pen and wrote an open letter, listing what to my mind were, and in hindsight still are, the main issues in the fashion system and outlining some possible solutions. The letter triggered a veritable movement of thoughts and ideas as well as a debate that embraced the entire system, and not just that. The news was picked up by everyone, and it also touched the public that does not work in the fashion industry. I received countless messages in response: from colleagues as well as from ordinary citizens; from clients and from people who aren't at all interested in fashion. This convinced me that telling it like it is, without filters, even saying things that aren't the nicest to hear, is the best way to communicate, especially so today, when many seem, more than anything else, busy in attracting attention with the stories they tell, stories that want to impress. This open letter was a new way for me to compare my thoughts and ideas with those of others, but also to imagine the business, outlining a sort of programmatic manifesto. The letter is reproduced unabridged in the following pages. It is a document that set the terms for the ethics and aesthetics of my group, tracing the path we are on now and that we will continue to pursue with unwavering belief.

I am writing this open letter to WWD, *and in particular to Miles Socha and his collaborators Samantha Conti, Alessandra Turra, and Luisa Zargani, in regards to the excellent piece "Will the Flood of Collections Yield to Slower Fashion?" published yesterday, April 2.*

Congratulations: the reflection on how absurd the current state of things is, with the overproduction of garments and a criminal nonalignment between the weather and the commercial season, is courageous and necessary. I agree with each and every point of it, in solidarity with the opinions expressed by my colleagues.

For years I have been raising the same questions during press conferences following my shows, often unheard or considered moralistic. The current emergency, on the other hand, shows that a careful and intelligent slowdown is the only way out, a road that will finally bring value back to our work and that will make final customers perceive its true importance and value.

The decline of the fashion system as we know it began when the luxury segment adopted the operating methods of fast fashion, mimicking the latter's endless delivery cycle in the hope of selling more, yet forgetting that luxury takes time, to be achieved and to be appreciated. Luxury cannot and must not be fast. It makes no sense for one of my jackets or suits to live in the shop for three weeks before becoming obsolete, replaced by new goods that are not too different.

I don't work like that, and I find it immoral to do so. I have always believed in an idea of timeless elegance, which is not only a precise aesthetic code but also an approach to the design and making of garments that suggests a way of buying them: to make them last. For the same reason, I find it absurd that, in the middle of winter, one can only find linen dresses in the shops and alpaca coats in the summer, for the simple reason that the desire to purchase must be satisfied immediately.

Who buys an item to put it in the closet waiting for the right season? None or just a few, I believe. But this, driven by department stores, has become the dominant mind-set, which I think is wrong and needs to change.

This crisis is an opportunity to slow down and realign everything; to define a more meaningful landscape. I have been working with my teams for three weeks so that, after the lockdown, the summer collections will remain in the boutiques at least until the beginning of September, as it is natural. And so we will do from now on.

This crisis is also an opportunity to restore value to authenticity: enough with fashion as pure communication, enough with cruise shows around the world to present mild ideas and to entertain with grandiose shows that today seem a bit inappropriate, and even a tad vulgar—enormous but ultimately meaningless wastes of money. Special events should happen for special occasions, not as a routine.

The moment we are going through is turbulent, but it also offers us the unique opportunity to fix what is wrong, to regain a more human dimension. It's nice to see that in this sense we are all united.

For retail this will be an important stress test. I want to send my heartfelt encouragement to the American fashion operators for the difficult weeks they will face ahead. United, we will make it. But we have to be united and operate in unison: this is perhaps the most important lesson we can learn from this crisis.

CLEAR THINKING

We talked a lot during the toughest days of the lockdown, and then later. The pandemic took away two whole years of our lives: an event that has been, in any case, shocking, reminding us just how small and fragile we are—in the end, just a small cog in the wheel of nature's immense system. An event that reminded me, with some differences no doubt, of the hard times of my childhood: years of restrictions and the fear of not surviving.

We talked a lot, those of us in fashion, one of the most important industries, both in Italy and elsewhere, but also one of the most polluting, based as it is on the irresponsible production and circulation of merchandise. We sought new solutions for a better future: less wasteful, less outrageous, more respectful of the planet. We sought to rationalize and also to moralize, overturning the absurdities and nonsense that over the years have become our way of doing things. This way of doing things is profoundly wrong, and it has caused considerable damage. However, now, as I write, exactly two years after the start of the pandemic, I see that, in spite of all the words that have been said, not much has changed. Actually, nothing at all has changed: the same exponential number of collections, the same desire to be there, the same fashion shows presented with a great deployment of means. We have gone back to exactly where we were before, perhaps with even greater anxiety, as if to make up for a period when we couldn't do any of those things. I did my bit as well, staging a fashion show in Dubai to celebrate the tenth anniversary of our Armani Hotel. But after that event, which, among other things, we made every effort to ensure it would have the smallest impact possible on the environment, I stopped and I did nothing else: it was a celebration that had been in the works for years, and I wanted to bring the project to fruition.

As for the rest, I try to remain a clear thinker, to see things for what they are, to act according to my conscience. The shock of the pandemic taught me a very important lesson and I have no intention of forgetting it. It is typical of human nature to do so, but it is equally human to evolve, which is what interests me. So I am committed to keeping faith with what was said at that moment, to follow the path traced in the programmatic manifestos and in the statements that succeeded one another. At this point in my life and career, it is also a way to leave behind a personal legacy and a method on which the Gruppo Armani can base itself in the future, when I am no longer here. Care for the planet, people, and the community are the cornerstones of this way of thinking. Without fanfare, without sensationalism. By doing, and nothing more, with the lucidity and the pragmatism that have always set me apart. The world is filled with words, but it is the actions, the facts, that speak.

LESS

I know that this concept can seem difficult, maybe even a paradox, when it comes from someone who creates fashion, where people are invited to buy more and more, to change their minds every six months, to have an endless number of options instead of just a few. But I am convinced that less is always better. I am borrowing this definition from the industrial designer Dieter Rams because I find it to be perfect: *less but better*. This is not a minimalist credo, also because I hardly identify with pre-established definitions or with generalized schools of thought, seeing that I have always been my own person. In minimalism there is something crude and forcibly sacrificial that is very distant from me and from my way of being, even though I prefer essential lines and keep decorations to a minimum. The fact is that my essentialness is designed to follow the body and its movements: it is not an aesthetic challenge, but, rather, the quest for naturalness, for continuity between the outfit and the person. And here I go back to my original thought: less but better. Do we really need lots of stuff? Must we really fulfill every whim? Must we live surrounded by things? I don't think so. It's not good for us, it's not good for the mind, it's not good for the planet where we live. I received this imprinting as a child and it is indelible: although we didn't have much at home, we still had everything we needed. Most importantly, there was no lack of dignity. When you don't have a lot, you give it your all, you find solutions, you invent things. The ideal wardrobe, for me, is a distillate of timeless clothes that men and women can combine, each time, in the way that best represents them at that particular moment. Beautiful things have no expiration date. They don't suddenly turn ugly at the end of the season; quite the contrary, they acquire beauty and personality over the years. All of my work is based on this idea, on a subtle, I would say almost millimetric evolution of classic garments, of modernity made to stand the test of time. This philosophy of living and dressing is, to use a common expression today, sustainable, because it invites us to recycle and not to waste. But such a philosophy has always been mine. My quest for less and better was also the path to a great professional conquest. It is generally said that classics are timeless. My language has represented and continues to represent modernity in dressing, but it is also timeless, ergo my modernity is timeless. It is made up of less, and it is better. It is a sign that I am proud of, because it harkens back to the classical ideal according to which what is beautiful must also be good.

RESPONSIBILITY

Beautiful as good, I have often repeated in this book. I am firmly convinced of this: ethics and aesthetics can in no way be separated. In particular, beauty cannot be produced to the detriment of the planet where we live, which is one and which we must hand over as intact as possible to the generations that come after us. Just as we must hand over intact, and as green as possible, the cities where we live, imagining more harmonious dimensions of living and on a human scale. I have always personally been very sensitive to the environment, but transforming all this into a way of doing the fashion business, hence, from start to finish, is a path I undertook, with great passion and devotion, only relatively recently,

much like everyone else. I believe that environmental awareness is the strongest school of thought to have emerged in
recent years. It is to the present time like the 1968 protests
were to the doctrines that were dominant back then. It is
a vital and all-encompassing thought that comes from the
grassroots and, in particular, from young people, involving all
of society and forcing everyone to open their eyes and, most
importantly, to act. The turnaround was very sharp: no one
could avoid it. The time for hemming and hawing, for sitting
on the fence has passed, because it could already be too late.
As concerns me personally, I am trying to make every aspect
of the Armani world as responsible as possible, fully aware
that it is often the small actions that, when added to other
small actions, achieve the greatest results. The process of
constant improvement I aim for goes through the production
chain, the involvement of suppliers, the choice of raw materials, but also the organization of events and a whole series
of donations aimed to benefit nature, whether in the city or
the green belts that are a guarantee of life itself on our planet.
These are just the first steps and the first attempts, no doubt,
but we have to start somewhere, so it is best to do so right
away and with conviction. I also realize that the risk in our
system, so inclined toward communicating, is dithering with
beautiful words instead of good deeds. While I don't have
broad solutions, I do have personal ones: in my group a sustainable division is hard at work in a rigorous and transversal

manner in every branch, in every aspect, not least of which is that of the philosophy of style and living. And in this as well I am committed to doing more than describing, because only by doing can we achieve results. It's hard for me to find the words to describe how distraught I am when I see images of natural destruction, and the suffering that this causes in the human beings who are the weakest. A long time ago, I as well experienced some of that malaise, and I will never forget it. For a successful man like me, giving back is not a good deed but rather a duty toward the community, a necessity that I cannot shirk. Society, understood as a global unity of all human beings, is like nature. We ourselves are the environment: it belongs to us and we belong to it. We should all do what it takes to make sure that our time on this planet is not an opportunity for destruction, but rather for construction.

STORYTELLING

I have lived a long enough life to be able to say with certainty that every era has its obsessions. Liberation defined the 1970s; spendthrift exhibitionism, the 1980s (I still recall the expression Reagan-era hedonism being used on *Quelli della notte*, an entertaining, satirical TV show conducted by Renzo Arbore); minimalist extremism, the 1990s, and so on. Today, with the advent of social media, there is a great deal of talk everywhere about what's known as storytelling. We all feel we need to tell other people things, both about our private lives and about work. We all have to transmit our lives in real time, endlessly, or it would be as if we weren't living at all. This is even more true for labels. It seems that telling stories and ideas is the only way to make old and new clients loyal, and to affirm one's own importance. My perplexity depends on my love of authenticity. I believe that, if the garments themselves don't tell the stories, then there's something amiss. In the field of fashion, I instead see stories circulating that, while aiming to be shared and inclusive especially, are often of little credibility. I cannot see any originality in these stories. What concerns me the most is that storytelling has gone from being a communications tool to being at the heart of everything. The way a label talks about itself is now the sole, true merchandise, while it is the product and that alone that can tell stories. For someone like me who has always communicated—and still does—in an honest and direct way, all this sounds like artifice. I don't want to be misunderstood: advertising needs fanciful stories because telling stories is a profound human urge. However, in fashion, and not just that, the narrative should exalt, not mystify. It should accompany, not confuse. What comes to mind is the black and white that I have always preferred to describe my timeless fashion, or the stories that are just hinted at by my shots: these are narratives that stimulate the public's imagination, rather than dumb it down. That said, I claim the right to declare that an object that is worn should talk and excite on its own. I, at least, have always worked in this direction. If you need to devise complicated stories, what remains of the force and the identity of the product being presented? All the problems that had been swept under the carpet will come out eventually, they always do, and even the most distracted public will understand if you really do have something to tell. Nothing is more powerful than the truth.

STANDING UP FOR SOMETHING AND PUTTING MY NAME TO IT

If I believe in something, standing up for something and putting my name to it comes naturally to me. I have done the same with many of my outfits, one of which is permanently on display at the entrance to the Silos. This was even more true, and in a way that was not at all frivolous, during the pandemic: an emergency that left us all naked, as human beings, exposing our deepest weaknesses. I acted instinctively and according to my conscience, spurred by the desire to be of use. I did this in many different ways: with donations to charities, with interventions in the poorer areas, and with other activities I don't want to mention, simply because I did so from the bottom of my heart, not for publicity reasons.

I know I'm privileged, but I'm human, and I was afraid, too, like everyone else. My duty is to give back to the community. I do so believing in it, and for this reason I have stood up for things and put my name to them. If I say something in the first person, exposing myself, then people feel I am close to them. And indeed the reaction by the entire public to such great exposure on my part was truly moving. Empathy is important: it unites us and brings us closer. I also wanted to illustrate this empathy in the mural space on Via Broletto, so I converted it from an advertising space to my open channel of communication with the public. First, I dedicated the huge wall to the image of the doctor who holds all of Italy in her arms, thus becoming the symbol of the fight against Covid-19. A heart-rending image and work by Franco Rivoli, a very moving one at that. Then, I again spoke in the first person, with my hand on my heart, on December 2020. Just a few, deeply sincere words, black on white, and all in caps: I AM HERE FOR MILAN, WITH THE MILANESE, WITH FEELING. Simply that. I will never tire of repeating that I always prefer facts to words, but these were words I wanted to say because I could feel them burning inside. Although I acted in favor of Milan, which is my city, I never forgot the rest of the country. For me, engaging directly was an incentive I could not resist. Am I despotic because I always want to make the final decision, and sign it, too? Perhaps. But it is also a way for me to shoulder my responsibilities, which I will not shirk.

FOLLOWING PAGES: MESSAGE OF SOLIDARITY WITH THE PEOPLE OF MILAN, MURAL ON VIA BROLETTO, DECEMBER 2020

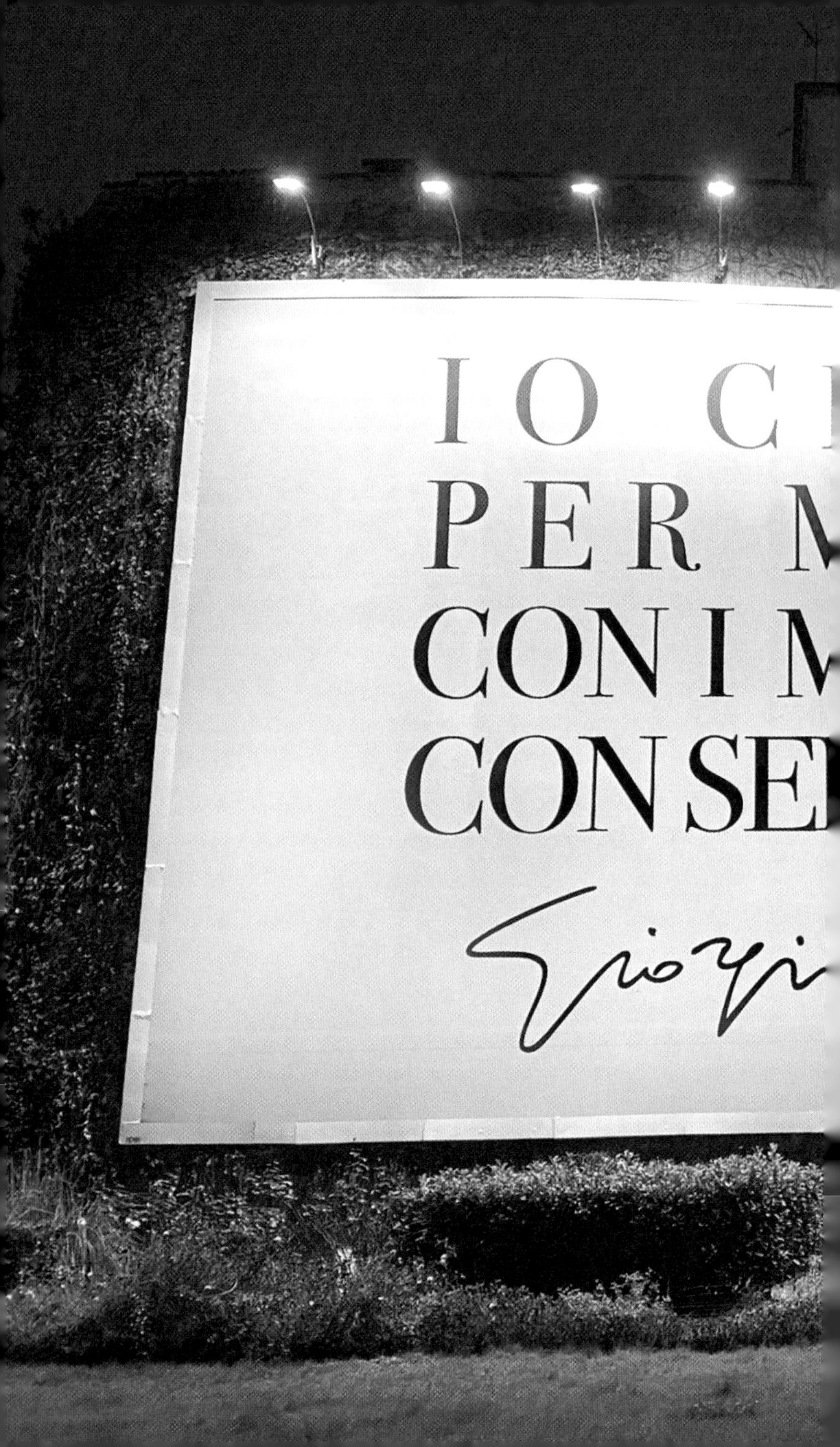
IO C
PER M
CON I M
CON SE

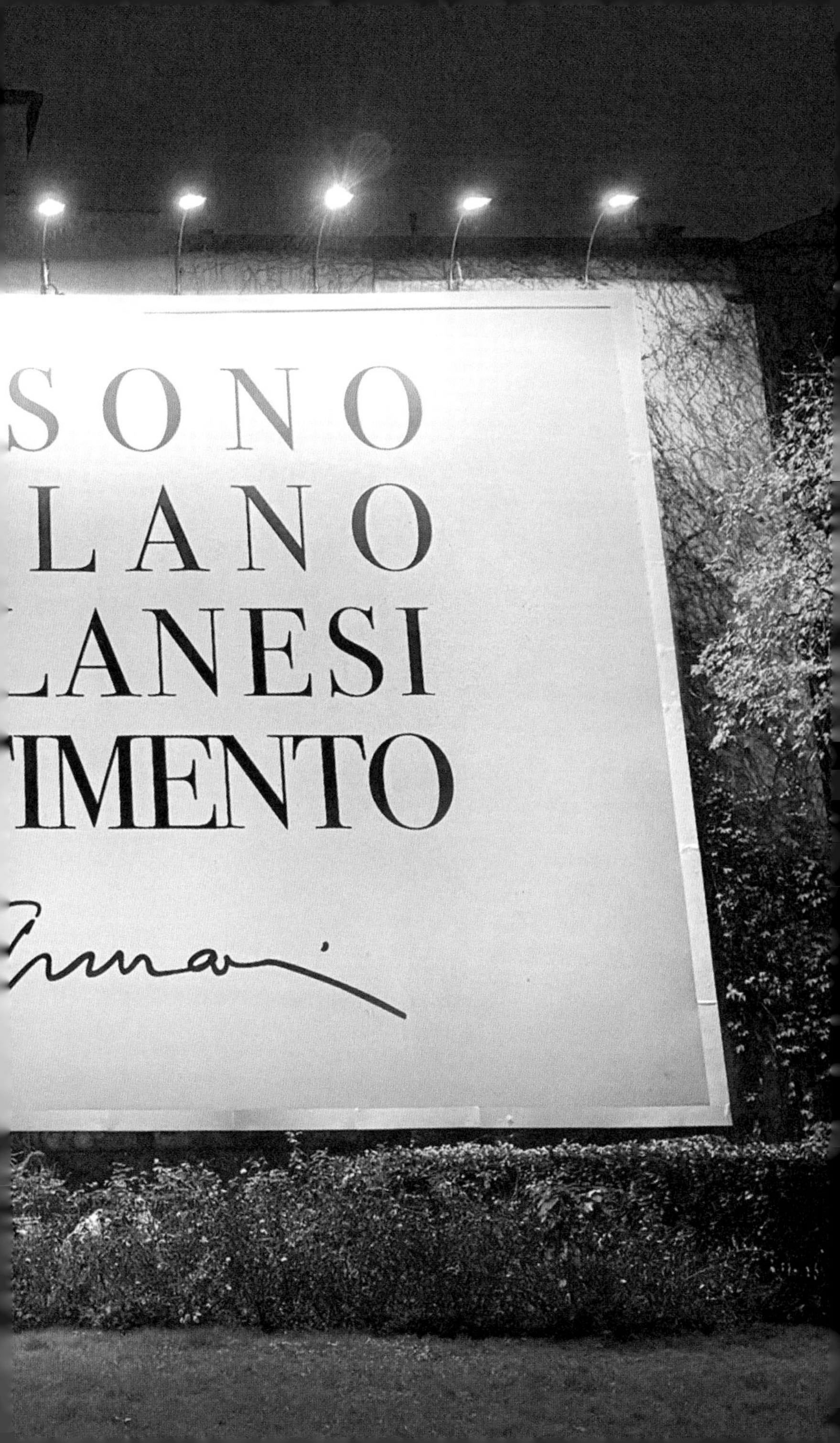
SONO
LANO
LANESI
IMENTO

MILAN

The world we are living in knows no bounds: it is open, global, constantly connected, and very fast. It is precisely for this reason that I believe nurturing one's roots is becoming increasingly important. Not for some foolish or anachronistic nationalistic feeling of belonging, as much as for our contribution—each of us in his own way and with his own original vision—to the exciting variety of the present. That's the way it is in fashion, too. Nowadays, for instance, we no longer talk about Italian style, as was the case when I made my debut. However, there definitely does exist a way that is completely and solely Italian in how the project of fashion is approached: a way that is both pragmatic and epicurean, that celebrates beauty as well as trade, with sobriety and discretion. It is a concrete but inspired way that concedes nothing to useless intemperance, on a male and female scale: industrious, practical, determined. For me, all this is Milan, which is why I am constantly looking to this city and feeling both appeased and stimulated, absorbing all its vital energy.

My relationship with Milan is a very strong, even intimate one. Milan is at the heart of my world, in every way possible. It is the city I chose, not only as a place to live, but as a way of living. I chose it precisely because of its energy, its strength, its willingness to start over again every morning knowing that work is what will lead to every possible solution.

I chose Milan when I was a boy and the Reconstruction was eliminating the scars of the war. I saw the city maimed by the bombs, poor, a city that with its desire to start over again had attracted my family. I chose Milan in that decade of unrest that was the 1970s, when terrorism did not seem to let up. From my first studio, two ground-floor rooms on Corso Venezia, I could hear the protesters marching past while I tried, one drawing after another, to imagine the prêt-à-porter style and the new society that would interpret it. I chose Milan as the place to build my life and my work, private and public, as the place where I and the world of Armani would live. And I continue to choose Milan every day because even when it trembles, it will not be shaken. Because it thinks about tomorrow while living today, without ever stopping. Because it does not know what it means to give up.

I see myself and I recognize myself in Milan, and that is why, in the hardest and darkest moments of these most recent years, I have constantly supported it, not only with messages of encouragement, but with actions and donations in favor of institutions as well. And there are many such institutions that make this city so welcoming, so altruistic, so attentive to everyone's needs despite its hard, austere facade. These are actions that I carry out and that I rarely communicate, for I feel it is simply my duty to do so.

But I have also exploited Milan's huge capacity for communication. In this sense, the city is very powerful. In the collective imaginary, and not just that of Italians, Milan represents modernity and industriousness. In my work I have chosen corners and partial views, but also symbolic places like Linate Airport, where, all by myself, I held an Emporio collection fashion show in 2018. The airport is a place of great and boundless beauty: it represents an openness toward the outside, toward the world. It is a place you depart from so you can learn and discover things, and it is a place you go back to after experiencing countless adventures. I liked the idea of organizing that event in the very same hangar where, since 1996, the words Emporio Armani have stood out, topped by the characteristic eagle logo: an iconic image that accompanies and welcomes thousands of travelers either leaving or arriving in the city. It is a message of freedom and cosmopolitanism, confirming Milan as the center of gravity in my world.

TELEVISION

Perhaps because I grew up at a time when mass communication was becoming widespread, even inspiring artists like Andy Warhol and pop art, I have always been fascinated by popular means that are capable of reaching the largest audience in the most immediate and direct way possible. These are means that today would appear to be analogic and slow, if compared to digital culture, which is instead incredibly fast and inclined to forgetfulness. Means that preserve and transmit strong emotions, which still cannot be found anywhere else. To my mind, if there is no emotion, then communication is incomplete. Without wanting to sound boastful, I was the first fashion designer to use billboards as a means of advertising when I chose to use the mural on Via Broletto in Milan to express Emporio Armani. Of course, the more popular brands were already doing so, but not the designer labels, and I was reprimanded for what I had done. Once again, there was no lack of criticism and skeptical objections, but as always I continued straight down my path and the success of my idea with the public proved to me that I was right. I am very proud of the Spring/Summer 2021 fashion show, aired on TV during prime-time on a Saturday night, because I basically offered everyone a front-row seat, breaking the mold of elitism typical of the fashion world. I made a pop-nationalist choice in the most positive sense of the term: choosing television to unveil a new collection means having reached a truly vast audience, without snobbishness. And all this, as always, without compromising my sense of style, without adulterating it. Once again, the reaction was strong, transversal. Holding a fashion show on television really does open the door to everyone, much more than doing so on the Internet. No one is excluded. That gesture made me stronger because my taste is anything but pop nationalist. On the contrary, it is purified, whispered. It clashes with the flamboyant, over-the-top excess of certain TV shows. But I tell my style to everyone, and I believe this is the secret to my success. I create a world of aspirations in which rich does not rhyme with uncouth, golden, or glittery, but rather with toned down, intimate, suspended. I suggest a communion between what is beautiful and what is good, in clothes as well as in words, and I express this unfiltered and without excluding anyone. I made my way up from the bottom and consider myself a self-made man. I am well aware that style and elegance are everywhere, not only in the upper social classes. This is my idea of democracy and inclusion, words that are so fashionable in today's narratives. But too often they are merely cunning refrains.

FOLLOWING PAGES: EMPORIO ARMANI, FALL/WINTER 1991–1992, POSTER WITH THE PICTURE *LUNCH ATOP A SKYSCRAPER, ROCKEFELLER CENTER* BY CHARLES C. EBBETS, 1932

HONORS

Throughout my career I have received a great number of awards and acknowledgments from around the world. In 1983 the Council of Fashion Designers of America named me *International Designer of the Year*, and from that moment on the honors have never stopped coming: Commendatore della Repubblica in 1985, Grand'Ufficiale dell'Ordine al Merito della Repubblica in 1986, Gran Cavaliere della Repubblica in 1987, honorary degrees from the Brera Academy and the Politecnico in Milan, the Royal College of Art and Central Saint Martins in London, the French Légion d'honneur in 2008, and even a day dedicated to me in New York— October 24, 2013—at the behest of the then mayor, Michael Bloomberg. Lastly, in 2021, I was awarded the title Cavaliere di Gran Croce dell'Ordine al Merito by President Sergio Mattarella: the Republic of Italy's highest and most prestigious

GIORGIO ARMANI AFTER RECEIVING AN HONORARY
DEGREE FROM MILAN POLITECNICO, 2007

honor, a title that is conferred with a presidential decree for the highest merits. What can I say? I'm proud of every single one, and I would be a hypocrite if I said I wasn't. But I'm keeping my feet firmly planted on the ground and my eyes laser-focused. I am truly proud to represent the finest values of our country in the world: what this means is that what I do does not go unnoticed, and that the institutions, not only the public, recognize this. It is the reward, each time renewed and reiterated, for my untiring commitment, and for the work of those who are close to me. I am proud of and grateful for every single acknowledgment, but, to be honest, I have never actually counted them. I keep some of them in my home, some of them in my studio, never too much out in the open, because, for me, they are very personal, almost private, even though they come from all kinds of institutions. The feeling with which I look upon all these successes is—I have to be honest—the same as always. It is the same feeling that got me this far: you can always do more and better, without resting on your laurels. I wouldn't call this insatiability; perhaps restlessness is a better word. No doubt it is a dynamic push. So, yes, I'm satisfied, but I want to go further, I want to take up new challenges. I am also mindful of Dante's warning that "the wind smites most upon the loftiest summits." I want to set an example, for the things that I do, not for the success that is a result of what I do, although I am aware of the fact that success does make up for all the effort made.

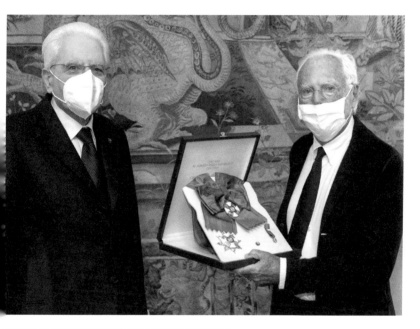

GIORGIO ARMANI RECEIVES THE HONORARY TITLE OF CAVALIERE
DI GRAN CROCE FROM PRESIDENT MATTARELLA, NOVEMBER 2021

AFTER

A career spanning almost fifty years: the achievement of a great target. It seems like yesterday that I first began, filled with enthusiasm, determination, ideas, and instead here I am today. The enthusiasm is still the same, as is the determination, and I'm still full of ideas. Maybe I have a few extra aches and pains, but my white hair and limpid gaze are the same as they were before and always have been.

I am a man of facts, a designer of challenges, an entrepreneur of conquests: I only look forward, with no nostalgia and no self-satisfaction about what I have achieved, always ready to venture down new roads. And that is why it is hard for me to come to a conclusion. Once one show is over, I'm already

GIORGIO ARMANI WOMEN'S COLLECTION,
SPRING/SUMMER 2023

thinking about the next one. Once a successful handbag has been designed, I'm imagining the one that will follow. After opening a hotel or a café, I'm committed to opening another one that's better than the first one. When a campaign begins, I'm already hard at work experimenting with a new kind of communication. Having dressed the actors in a movie, I'm busy reading the scripts to decide which new production I want to participate in. That's just the way I am.

This book as well, which is a collection of thoughts and actions, is hard for me to finish: I imagined it as something that flowed and that every reader could follow as they wished, without a true beginning or end. It can be read from the last page to the first, or the other way around, or it can be read by skipping from one page to another. It is a fluid, multifaceted document, just like my fashion. I hate the idea of adding a period and then writing "the end," but I realize that I have no choice but to do so. I, too, will one day have to give up my command and end my work as a fashion designer: this will not happen anytime soon, but I have been thinking about it for some time now because I want the results of all my efforts—this company to which I have given my whole life and all my energy—to go forward for a long time, even without me. I have drafted my plan for succession, with my usual pragmatism and great discretion, but I am not going to tell anyone about it now for the simple fact that I'm still here. It is for this very reason that I have created my Foundation.

To all those who wonder about this burning topic, all I can say is that, yes, there will be an Armani after Armani, curated by the people who are around me now, by the collaborators who are a part of my ideal family today. They are beside me each and every day, impassioned and determined the way I want them to be. To them, to all those who are close to me, but above all to my public, I dedicate this book, which I hope is filled with ideas and suggestions, with food for thought and a feast for the eyes. It is not a handbook—that is not how I imagined it to be. However, I would like such a unique document to serve as a spark for readers who leaf through it: encouraging them to act, express themselves, invent. Not necessarily to go into fashion, which is perhaps already too crowded a field, but rather to find a pathway for their own life and to follow it with passion. That is the only lesson I will allow myself to teach. Thirty years ago, to those who interviewed me, I would say that I couldn't imagine myself at the age of eighty still at the head of the company. But instead, here I am: not because I am trying to hold on, but because I enjoy it and because work keeps you young, in thought and in spirit. When you do things with your heart and your mind, when you invent something while getting involved personally, the variable of time is only relative.

Allow me to conclude: I have commitments that await me, and I've already gone on long enough. The finale is an open-ended one. I shall continue to work . . .

PER AMORE

Just one final, very short thought: I really find it hard to finish. I am certain that anyone who picks up this book will be surprised by the title, which is so soft, even romantic, sentimental. So un-Armani-like, after all. These are not the features that are generally associated with me. In the public eye I am composed, determined, stern, and, for some, terribly cold. I am old enough not to have to explain my way of being, and in any case I have never done so because you are what you are. But I like to think of myself by borrowing a definition from the painter Wassily Kandinsky: I'm like a piece of ice with a flame burning inside. I'm someone who uses his head, who thinks, but my actions all come from the heart, they are inflamed with passion. There, I'm hot-blooded, and that's why these random thoughts gathered here were written per amore*. For the love of what? Of expression, of vision, of taste, of style. It all comes from within, from an idea, and from the burning desire to make it come true. Every idea, after all, is an act of falling in love. Putting it forward and reiterating it without allowing it to be too influenced by passing fads, by the distractions that abound, requires endless love. This work that is my life is a never-ending act of love, and conveying it to my public in such an intimate and direct form is as well. And now I really will end this with one last period.*

For the time being, at least.

CONTENTS

9 | PREFACE

13 | ME, IN MY OWN WORDS

75 | MY BYWORDS,
     FOR EVERYONE TO USE

GIORGIO ARMANI
IN BEIJING, 2004

ACKNOWLEDGMENTS

Thank you to Angelo Flaccavento for his collaboration.

All the revenues accruing from the royalties for this book
will be donated by Giorgio Armani to Save the Children Italia Onlus.

Graphic design: Laura Decaminada
Translation: Sylvia Notini

© 2022 Mondadori Libri S.p.A.
Distributed in English throughout the World
by Rizzoli International Publications Inc.
300 Park Avenue South
New York, NY 10010, USA

ISBN: 978-88-918372-0-2

2023 2024 2025 2026 / 10 9 8 7 6 5 4 3 2 1

First edition: May 2023

This volume was printed at L.E.G.O. S.p.A., Vicenza
Printed in Italy

Visit us online:
Facebook.com/RizzoliNewYork
Twitter: @Rizzoli_Books
Instagram.com/RizzoliBooks
Pinterest.com/RizzoliBooks
Youtube.com/user/RizzoliNY
Issuu.com/Rizzoli

MIX
Paper | Supporting
responsible forestry
FSC® C023419